TWO *Simple* SHAPES =

26 Crocheted Cardigans, Tops & Sweaters

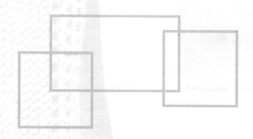

SALENA BACA

STACKPOLE BOOKS
Guilford, Connecticut

Published by Stackpole Books
An imprint of The Rowman & Littlefield Publishing Group, Inc.
4501 Forbes Blvd., Ste. 200
Lanham, MD 20706
www.stackpolebooks.com

Distributed by NATIONAL BOOK NETWORK
800-462-6420

British Library Cataloguing in Publication Information available

Library of Congress Cataloging-in-Publication Data available

Names: Baca, Salena, author.
Title: Two simple shapes = 26 crocheted cardigans, tops & sweaters : if you
    can crochet a square and rectangle, you can make these easy-to-wear
    designs! / Salena Baca.
Other titles: Two simple shapes = twenty-six crocheted cardigans, tops &
    sweaters | Two simple shapes = 26 crocheted cardigans, tops and sweaters |
    Two simple shapes equals 26 crocheted cardigans, tops & sweaters
Description: First edition. | Guilford, Connecticut : Stackpole Books, [2019]
    | Includes index.
Identifiers: LCCN 2018055407| ISBN 9780811737838 (pbk. : alk. paper) | ISBN
    9780811767712 (e-book)
Subjects: LCSH: Crocheting—Patterns. | Sweaters. | Women's clothing.
Classification: LCC TT825 .B2938 2019 | DDC 746.43/40432—dc23 LC record
available at https://lccn.loc.gov/2018055407

♾™ The paper used in this publication meets the minimum requirements of
American National Standard for Information Sciences—Permanence of Paper
for Printed Library Materials, ANSI/NISO Z39.48-1992.

First Edition

Printed in the United States of America

Contents

Introduction

Simple squares and rectangles can easily be constructed to create shawls, ponchos, pullovers, cocoon vests, and so much more. Since the shapes are kept simple, these patterns are the perfect playground for learning and practicing new-to-you stitches. Playing with these two basic forms as a theme, the creative crochet artists who contributed designs to *Two Simple Shapes* have produced a collection of gorgeous, easy-to-wear, timeless designs!

Each design in *Two Simple Shapes* has been paired with a trusted Lion Brand yarn, using plush colors and alluring patterns to create pieces that you'll wear for years to come!

Peace + Love + Crochet
Salena

THE PATTERNS

24/7 Vest

Designed by Salena Baca

This light vest works great as a spring and summer accessory! The style is easy to work up, and it complements a range of body shapes too.

SKILL LEVEL
Intermediate

SIZES/FINISHED MEASUREMENTS
Small (Medium, Large)
Length: 18 (20, 22) in./45.5 (51, 56) cm
Width: 25.5 (30, 34.5) in./64.5 (76, 87.5) cm

YARN
Lion Brand Yarn 24/7 Cotton, medium weight #4 yarn
    (100% mercerized cotton; 186 yd./170 m per 3.5 oz./
    100 g skein)
  ▪ 2 (3, 3) skeins Taupe 122

HOOK AND OTHER MATERIALS
  ▪ US size J-10 (6.0 mm) crochet hook
  ▪ Yarn needle

GAUGE
10 sts in pattern = 4 in./10 cm
2 rows in pattern = 1.5 in./4 cm
Adjust hook size if necessary to obtain gauge.

NOTES
  ▪ Similar #4 weight yarns may be substituted; please
    check gauge.
  ▪ Pattern is written in four sections: Back Panel, 2
    Side Panels, Border.
  ▪ Turning chains do not count as a st.
  ▪ Vest style should be open about 10 in./25 cm in
    front. For best fit, measure under arms and around
    bust; follow size with width that is about 10 in./
    25 cm smaller than bust measurement.

INSTRUCTIONS

Back Panel

Ch 47 (52, 57).

Row 1: Hdc into third ch from hook and in each ch across, turn—45 (50, 55) hdc.

Row 2 (RS): Ch 4, tr in each st across, turn—45 (50, 55) tr.

Row 3: Ch 2, hdc in each st across, turn—45 (50, 55) hdc.

Repeat *Rows 2 and 3* until 21 (23, 25) rows complete; do not fasten off.

Side Panels

Right Panel

Row 1: Ch 4, tr in next 20 sts, turn—20 tr.

Row 2: Ch 2, hdc in each st across—20 hdc.

Repeat *Rows 1 and 2* until 6 (8, 10) rows complete; fasten off.

Left Panel

With RS of Back Panel facing, skip 25 (30, 35) sts of Row 1; attach yarn.

Repeat *Rows 1 and 2* of Right Panel, until 6 (8, 10) rows complete; fasten off.

Border

With RS of Panels facing, join yarn to first st of Right Panel.

Row 1: Ch 1, sc in next 20 sts, ch 25, sc in each row end of Back Panel, ch 25, sc in next 20 sts of Left Panel, turn—61 (63, 65) sc, 2 ch-25 spaces.

Row 2: Ch 2, hdc in each st across, turn—111 (113, 115) hdc.

Row 3: Ch 1, sc in each st across, turn—111 (113, 115) sc.

Row 4: Repeat *Row 2.*

Row 5: Repeat *Row 3.*

Fasten off.

Finishing

Weave in ends.

Fringe

Cut 5 pieces of yarn 20 in./51 cm for each fringe bundle. Evenly knot 1 bundle to each hdc row end of Border, and each tr row end from Back, Right, and Left Panels.

Cold-Shoulder Granny Square

Designed by Salena Baca

This may look like a simple granny square, but the cold-shoulder style gives this top an ultramodern look!

SKILL LEVEL
Intermediate

SIZES/FINISHED MEASUREMENTS
Small (Medium, Large)
Bust: 42 (46, 50) in./106.5 (117, 127) cm
Panel width: 21 (23, 25) in./53 (58, 63.5) cm
Panel height: 21 (23, 25) in./53 (58, 63.5) cm

YARN
Lion Brand Yarn Superwash Merino, light weight #3
 yarn (100% superwash merino wool; 306 yd./280 m
 per 3.5 oz./100 g skein)
- 3 (3, 4) skeins Charcoal 149

HOOK AND OTHER MATERIALS
- US size J-10 (6.0 mm) crochet hook
- Stitch markers
- Yarn needle

GAUGE
15 dc and 4 rows = 4 in./10 cm
Adjust hook size if necessary to obtain gauge.

NOTES
- Similar #3 weight yarns may be substituted; please
  check gauge.
- Pattern is constructed using two square panels
  and then seamed at the end.

INSTRUCTIONS

Body Panel (make 2)

Make adjustable loop/ring.

Round 1: Ch 6 (counts as dc, ch-3 here and throughout), [dc, ch 1, dc, ch 3] 3 times in ring, dc in ring, ch 1, sl st to third ch of beginning ch-6 to join—8 dc, 4 corner ch-3 spaces, 4 ch-1 spaces.

Round 2: Sl st in next 2 ch, ch 6, dc in same space, [ch 1, dc in next dc, dc in next ch-1 space, dc in next dc, ch 1, (dc, ch 3, dc) in corner ch-3 space] 3 times, ch 1, dc in next dc, dc in next ch-1 space, dc in next dc, ch 1, sl st to third ch of beginning ch-6 to join—20 dc, 4 corner ch-3 spaces, 8 ch-1 spaces.

Round 3: Sl st in next 2 ch, ch 6, dc in same space, [ch 1, dc in next dc, dc in each dc across side, dc in next ch-1 space, dc in next dc, ch 1, (dc, ch 3, dc) in corner ch-3 space] 3 times, ch 1, dc into next dc, dc into next ch-1 space, dc in each dc across side, dc into next ch-1 space, dc in next dc, ch 1, sl st to third ch of beginning ch-6 to join—36 dc, 4 corner ch-3 spaces, 8 ch-1 spaces.

Rounds 4–20 (22, 24): Repeat *Round 3*, each repeat of Round adds 16 dc to stitch count, but the 4 corner ch-3 spaces and 8 ch-1 spaces remain constant throughout.

Last Round: Sl st in next 2 ch, ch 6, dc in same space, *[ch 1, skip 1 st, dc into next] 40 (44, 48) times across side, ch 1, skip 1 st*, (dc, ch 3, dc) in corner ch-3 space; repeat from * around ending last repeat at *, sl st to third ch of beginning ch-6 to join—168 (184, 200, 216) dc, 176 (192, 208, 224) ch.

Fasten off.

Seams

Small (Medium, Large)
(Seam instructions differ per size.)
With RS of Body Panel 1 facing, skip 13 dc on any side; attach yarn.

Right Seam

Row 1: Ch 4 (counts as dc, ch-1 here and throughout), skip 1 st, [dc in next, ch 1, skip 1 st] 18 times, dc into next st, turn—20 dc, 19 ch-1 spaces.
Row 2: Ch 4, skip 1 st, [dc in next, ch 1, skip 1 st] 18 times, dc into last st—20 dc, 19 ch-1 spaces.
Fasten off.

Left Seam

Repeat instructions from Right Seam.

Neck Seam

4 parts create cold-shoulder tabs.

Tab:
Row 1: Ch 4, skip 1 st, [dc in next, ch 1, skip 1 st] 2 times, dc into next st, turn—4 dc, 3 ch-1 spaces.
Row 2: Ch 4, skip 1 st, [dc in next, ch 1, skip 1 st] 2 times, dc into last st, turn—4 dc, 3 ch-1 spaces.
Fasten off.
Skip 5 (7, 9) dc. Repeat instructions from Tab.
Skip 18 dc. Repeat instructions from Tab.
Skip 5 (7, 9) dc. Repeat instructions from Tab.

Finishing

With WS of Body Panels together, use stitch markers to align and hold seams evenly. With yarn needle, sew each seam to opposite Body Panel, evenly.

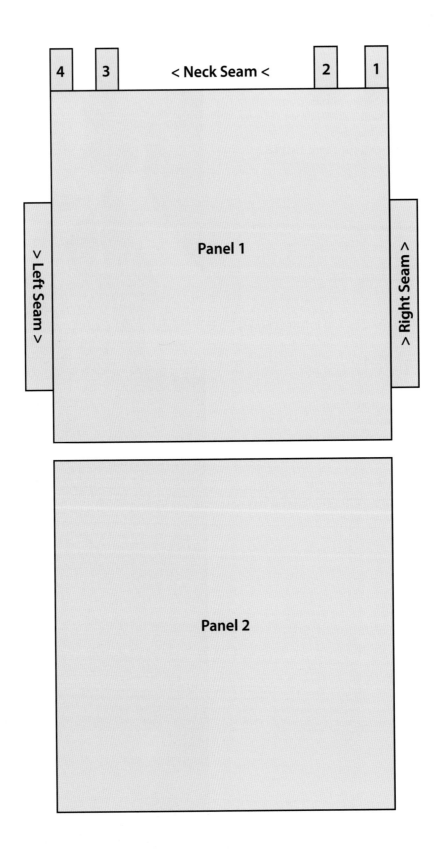

Falling Leaves Super Scarf

Designed by Salena Baca

A few simple increases and decreases create this openwork effect. This supersized scarf works up light and cozy in Jeans yarn, and the colors transform this piece into an everyday accessory!

SKILL LEVEL
Intermediate

SIZES/FINISHED MEASUREMENTS
12.5 in./32 cm wide x 85 in./216 cm long, before fringe

YARN
Lion Brand Yarn Jeans, medium weight #4 yarn (100% acrylic; 246 yd./225 m per 3.5 oz./100 g skein)
- 4 skeins Vintage 150

HOOK AND OTHER MATERIALS
- US size I-9 (5.5 mm) crochet hook
- Measuring tape
- Yarn needle

GAUGE
16.5 sts and 6.25 rows = 4 in./10 cm
Adjust hook size if necessary to obtain gauge.

SPECIAL STITCHES
Dc2tog (double crochet 2 stitches together). [Yo and insert hook in next st, yo and pull up loop, yo and pull through 2 loops] twice, yo and pull through all loops (decrease 2 sts).
Dc3tog (double crochet 3 stitches together). [Yo and insert hook in next st, yo and pull up loop, yo and pull through 2 loops] 3 times, yo and pull through all loops (decrease 3 sts).

NOTE
- Similar #4 weight yarns may be substituted; please check gauge.

INSTRUCTIONS

Ch 54.

Row 1 (RS): Dc2tog beginning in fourth ch from hook (skipped chs do not count as a st), [ch 2, skip 3 chs, 5 dc in next st, ch 2, skip 3 chs, dc3tog] 4 times, ch 2, skip 3 chs, 5 dc in next st, ch 2, skip 3 chs, dc2tog, turn—51 sts here and throughout.

Row 2: Ch 3 (not a st, here and throughout), [dc in next st, ch 1, skip ch-2 space, 2 dc in next dc, dc in next 3 dc, 2 dc in next dc, ch 1, skip ch-2 space] 5 times, dc in last st, turn.

Row 3: Ch 3, [dc, ch 2, skip ch-1 space, dc2tog, dc in next 3 sts, dc2tog, ch 2, skip ch-1 space] 5 times, dc in last st, turn.

Row 4: Ch 3, 3 dc in first st, [ch 1, skip ch-2 space, dc2tog, dc in next st, dc2tog, ch 1, skip ch-2 space, 5 dc in next st] 4 times, ch 1, skip ch-2 space, dc2tog, dc in next st, dc2tog, ch 1, skip ch-2 space, 3 dc in last st, turn.

Row 5: Ch 3, dc in first 2 sts, 2 dc in next, [ch 1, skip ch-1 space, dc3tog, ch 1, skip ch-1 space, 2 dc in next st, dc in next 3 sts, 2 dc in next st] 4 times, ch 1, skip ch-1 space, dc3tog, ch 1, skip ch-1 space, 2 dc in next st, dc in last 2 sts, turn.

Row 6: Ch 3, dc in first 2 sts, dc2tog, [ch 2, skip ch-1 space, dc in next st, ch 2, skip ch-1 space, dc2tog, dc in next 3 sts, dc2tog] 4 times, ch 2, skip 1 st, dc in next st, ch 2, skip ch-1 space, dc2tog, dc in last 2 sts, turn.

Row 7: Ch 3, dc in first st, dc2tog, [ch 3, skip ch-2 space, dc in next st, ch 3, skip ch-2 space, dc2tog, dc in next st, dc2tog] 4 times, ch 3, skip ch-2 space, dc in next st, ch 3, skip ch-2 space, dc2tog, dc in last st, turn.

Row 8: Ch 3, dc2tog, [ch 2, skip ch-3 space, 5 dc in next st, ch 2, skip ch-3 space, dc3tog] 4 times, ch 2, skip ch-3 space, 5 dc in next st, ch 2, skip ch-3 space, dc2tog, turn.

Repeat *Rows 2–8* until 133 rows complete, ending on a *Row 7* repeat; continue to Border without fastening.

Border

*Ch-8 spaces will be for fringe.

Ch 1 (not a st), (sc, ch 8, sc) in same st, skip 1 st, [ch 4, skip ch-3 space, sc in next, ch 4, skip ch-3 space, sc in next, (sc, ch 8, sc) in next st, sc in next st] 4 times, ch 4, skip ch-3 space, sc in next, ch 4, skip ch-3 space, skip 1 st, (sc, ch 8, sc) in next st, rotate to work along the side of the scarf, (sc, ch 1) in each dc row end across long side, rotate to work into Row 1, (sc, ch 8, sc) in next, [ch 4, skip ch-3 space, sc in next, ch 4, skip ch-3 space, sc in next, (sc, ch 8, sc) in next st, sc in next st] 4 times, ch 4, skip ch-3 space, sc in next, ch 4, skip ch-3 space, (sc, ch 8, sc) in next, rotate to work along the side of the scarf, (sc, ch 1) in each

dc row end across long side, sl st to first sc to join. Fasten off and weave in ends.

Fringe

*Cut 20 pieces of yarn measuring 13 in./33 cm long. Fold pieces in half evenly, draw center into ch-8 space from Border and pull ends through center until a knot forms. Repeat from * for all 12 ch-8 spaces. Trim fringe evenly.

Graceful Green Poncho

Designed by Salena Baca

The metallic strand twisting through this yarn turns a simple poncho into a glamorous statement piece! The deep V neck is an attractive touch as well.

SKILL LEVEL
Easy

SIZES/FINISHED MEASUREMENTS
Small (Medium, Large, 1X, 2X)
Width: 30 (32, 34, 35, 36) in./76 (81, 86.5, 89, 91) cm
Length: 48 (52, 54, 60, 64) in./122 (132, 137, 152.5, 162.5) cm

YARN
Lion Brand Yarn Shawl in a Ball, medium weight #4 yarn (58% cotton, 39% acrylic, 3% other; 518 yd./473 m per 5.3 oz./150 g skein)
- 2 (3, 3, 3, 4) skeins Graceful Green 306

HOOK AND OTHER MATERIALS
- US size J-10 (6.0 mm) crochet hook
- Yarn needle

GAUGE
11.16 sts = 4 in./10 cm; 9 rows = 5 in./12.5 cm
Adjust hook size if necessary to obtain gauge.

NOTES
- Pattern is worked in one piece, and fabric is reversible.
- Beginning ch-1 does not count as a sc.
- Beginning ch-4 counts as first tr.
- For the best fit, measure across elbow to elbow; follow size with closest matching width.

INSTRUCTIONS

Ch 136 (146, 157, 167, 180).

Row 1: Sc in second ch from hook and in each ch across, turn—135 (145, 156, 166, 179) sc.

Row 2: Ch 4, tr in each st across, turn—135 (145, 156, 166, 179) tr.

Row 3: Ch 1, sc in each st across, turn—135 (145, 156, 166, 179) sc.

Repeat *Rows 2–3* until 27 (29, 31, 33, 35) rows complete and then end on a *Row 3* repeat.

Row 28 (30, 32, 34, 36): Ch 4, tr in next 48 (53, 57, 62, 67) sts, ch 39 (39, 42, 42, 45), skip 39 (39, 42, 42, 45) sts, tr in last 48 (53, 57, 62, 67) sts—96 (106, 114, 124, 134) tr, 1 ch-space.

Repeat *Rows 3 and 2* until 55 (59, 63, 67, 71) rows complete, and then end on a *Row 3.*

Fasten off after last row complete.

Weave in ends.

Pound of Love Poncho

Designed by Salena Baca

A pound of love can go a long way with this design; one skein completes any size. And the light and airy pattern means this poncho can hang year-round!

SKILL LEVEL
Easy

SIZES/FINISHED MEASUREMENTS
Small (Medium, Large, 1X, 2X)
Width: 24 (26, 28, 30, 32) in./61 (66, 71, 76, 81) cm
Length: 48 (52, 56, 60, 64) in./122 (132, 142, 152.5, 162.5) cm

YARN
Lion Brand Yarn Pound of Love, medium weight #4 yarn (100% premium acrylic; 1,020 yd./932 m per 16 oz./454 g skein)
- 1 skein Navy 109

HOOK AND OTHER MATERIALS
- US size M-13 (9.0 mm) crochet hook
- Yarn needle

GAUGE
10.3 sts and 8 rows = 4 in./10 cm
Adjust hook size if necessary to obtain gauge.

SPECIAL STITCH
Dc3tog (double crochet 3 stitches together). [Yo and insert hook into next st, yo and pull up loop, yo and pull through 2 loops on hook] 3 times, yo and pull through all 4 loops on hook.

NOTES
- Similar #4 weight yarns may be substituted; please check gauge.
- For best fit, measure around arms at bust; add at least 4 in./10 cm (for ease) and follow size with length that matches most closely.
- This pattern is worked in rows. Fabric is reversible.
- Beginning ch-1 and ch-2 do not count as first st.

INSTRUCTIONS

Ch 63 (69, 75, 81, 87).

Row 1: Sc in second ch from hook and in each ch across, turn—62 (68, 74, 80, 86) sc.

Row 2: Ch 2, dc in first, skip 1 st, 3 dc in next st, [skip 2 sts, 3 dc in next st] 19 (21, 23, 25, 27) times, skip 1 st, dc in last st, turn—62 (68, 74, 80, 86) dc.

Row 3: Ch 1, sc in each st across, turn—62 (68, 74, 80, 86) sc.

Row 4: Ch 2, dc in first, ch 1, [dc3tog, ch 2] 19 (21, 23, 25, 27) times, dc3tog, ch 1, dc in last st, turn—20 (22, 24, 26, 28) dc3tog, 2 dc.

Row 5: Ch 1, sc into each st across, turn—62 (68, 74, 80, 86) sc.

Repeat *Rows 2–5* until 97 (105, 113, 121, 129) rows complete, and then end with a *Row 5* repeat.

Finishing

Fasten off, leaving a 30 in./76 cm tail. Fold fabric in half evenly, lengthwise. Turn fabric, to work into left side (from first and last row, toward center fold). Using a yarn needle, sew fabric together on left side, leaving an 11 in./28 cm gap (head opening). Fasten off and weave in ends.

Blanket Wrap

Designed by Salena Baca

Scarfie yarn is bulky, warm, and surprisingly lightweight! This luxurious accessory is comfortable, so very elegant, and incredibly easy to work up.

SKILL LEVEL
Easy

SIZES/FINISHED MEASUREMENTS
75 in./190.5 cm wide x 30 in./76 cm tall, before fringe

YARN
Lion Brand Yarn Scarfie, bulky #5 weight yarn (78% acrylic, 22% wool; 312 yd./285 m per 5.3 oz./150 g skein)
- 5 skeins Cream/Black 201 (includes 1 skein for fringe)

HOOK AND OTHER MATERIALS
- US size L-11 (8.0 mm) crochet hook
- Yarn needle

GAUGE
10.7 sts and 9.8 rows = 4 in./10 cm
Adjust hook size if necessary to obtain gauge.

NOTES
- Pattern is reversible.
- Beginning ch-1 does not count as a st.

INSTRUCTIONS

Ch 201.

Row 1: Beginning in second ch from hook, [sc2tog, ch 1] 100 times, turn—200 sts.

Rows 2–74: Ch 1, [BLO sc2tog, ch 1] 100 times—200 sts. Fasten off.

Fringe

*Cut 10 pieces of yarn, measuring 20 in./51 cm long. Fold pieces in half evenly, draw each end into one sc row end and pull ends through center to form knot. Repeat from * across right and left sides of Wrap— 37 bundles of fringe on each side, 74 bundles total. Trim fringe evenly.

Finishing

Weave in all ends.

Heartland Poncho

Designed by Salena Baca

Heartland yarn is soft, with comfortable drape and luxuriously blended colorways. This piece features amazing texture to complement your favorite fall outfit!

SKILL LEVEL
Intermediate

SIZES/FINISHED MEASUREMENTS
Measurements before side paneling; side paneling adds 4 in./10 cm total width.
Small (Medium, Large)
Width: 24 (26, 28) in./61 (66, 71) cm
Front height: 25 (27, 29) in./63.5 (68.5, 73.5) cm
Back height: 27 (29, 30) in./68.5 (73.5, 76) cm

YARN
Lion Brand Yarn Heartland, medium #4 weight yarn (100% acrylic; 251 yd./230 m per 5 oz./142 g skein)
  - 4 (5, 6) skeins Mount Rainier 150

HOOK AND OTHER MATERIALS
  - US size J-10 (6.0 mm) crochet hook
  - Yarn needle

GAUGE
14 sts and 8 rows = 4 in./10 cm
Adjust hook size if necessary to obtain gauge.

NOTE
  - This pattern is worked in 4 sections: Front Panel, Back Panel, Side Panels, and Neck.

INSTRUCTIONS

Front Panel

Ch 86 (98, 110).

Row 1 (RS): Skip 1 ch (not a st), [sc in next, skip 2 ch, (dc, ch 2, dc, ch 2, dc) in next st, skip 2 ch] 14 (16,18) times, sc in last ch, turn—85 (97, 109) sts.

Row 2: Ch 5 (counts as dc, ch-2), dc in same st, [skip 1 dc, sc in next dc, skip 1 dc, (dc, ch 2, dc, ch 2, dc) in next sc] 13 (15, 17) times, skip 1 dc, sc in next dc, (dc, ch 2, dc) in last st, turn—85 (97, 109) sts.

Row 3: Ch 1 (not a st), sc in next, [(dc, ch 2, dc, ch 2, dc) in next sc, skip 1 dc, sc in next dc] 14 (16, 18) times, turn—85 (97, 109) sts.

Repeat *Rows 2 and 3* until 48 (52, 56) rows complete and then end on a repeat of *Row 3.*

Fasten off.

Back Panel

With RS Front Panel facing, attach yarn to first st of Row 1.

Row 1 (RS): [Sc in next, skip 2 sts, (dc, ch 2, dc, ch 2, dc) in next st, skip 2 sts] 4 (5, 6) times, sc, ch 35, skip 35 sts, [sc, skip 2 sts, (dc, ch 2, dc, ch 2, dc) in next st, skip 2 sts] 4 (5, 6) times, sc in last st, turn—85 (97, 109) sts.

Repeat *Rows 2 and 3 of Front Panel* until 52 (56, 60) rows complete; do not fasten off.

Side Panels

Left Side

Ch 1 (not a st), turn to work into left side of Panels.

Row 1: 2 sc in every sc row end across left side of Panels, turn—100 (108, 116) sc.

Rows 2–6: Ch 2 (not a st), hdc in each st across, turn— 100 (108, 116) hdc.

Fasten off after last row complete.

Right Side

With RS of Front Panel facing, attach yarn to last st of last row. Repeat *Rows 1–6 of Left Side Panel*; fasten off after last row complete.

Neck

With RS of Panels facing, join yarn to first ch of Back Panel.

Rounds 1–4 (RS): Ch 1 (not a st), sc in each st around, sl st to first sc to join—70 sc.

Fasten off.

Finishing

Weave in all ends.

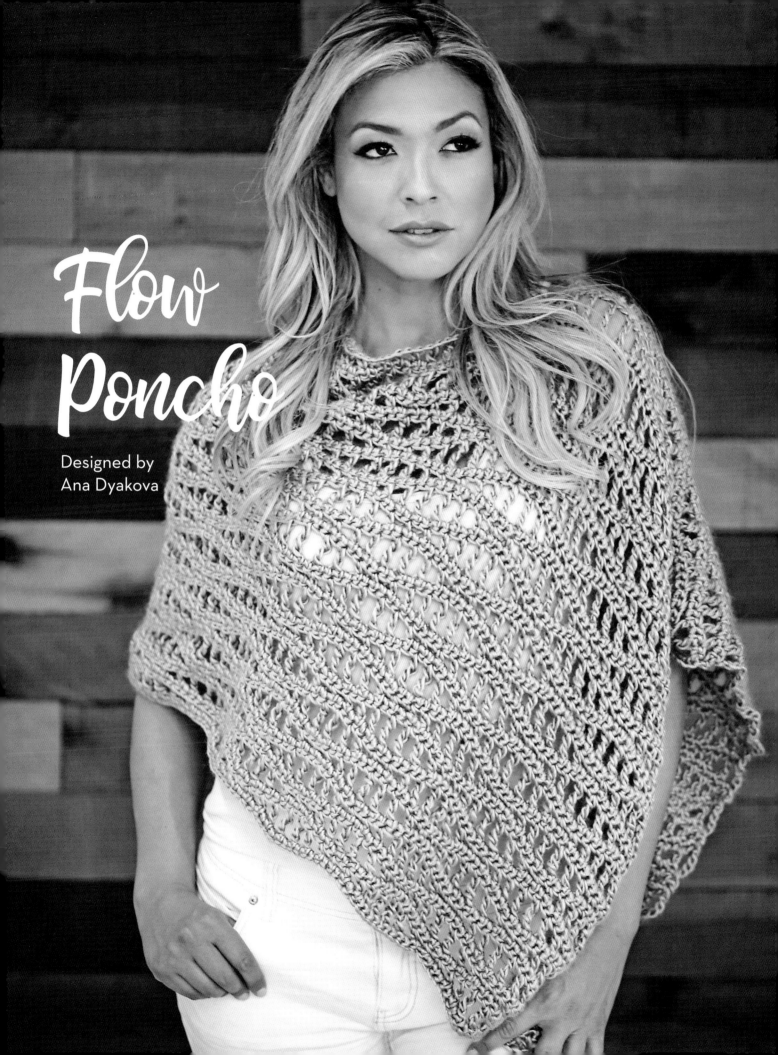

Flow Poncho

Designed by
Ana Dyakova

This cozy piece will hug you with a relaxed silhouette. It's light and airy, giving just the right amount of warmth!

SKILL LEVEL
Intermediate

SIZES/FINISHED MEASUREMENTS
Small (Medium, Large, 1X, 2X)
Width: 21 (21, 23.5, 26, 28.5) in./53 (53, 59.5, 66, 72.5) cm
Length: 54 (60, 66, 72, 78) in./137 (152.5, 167.5, 183, 198) cm

YARN
Lion Brand Yarn Amazing, medium weight #4 yarn
    (100% acrylic; 147 yd./134 m per 3.5 oz./100 g skein)
  - 4 (4, 5, 5, 6) skeins Silver 150

HOOK AND OTHER MATERIALS
  - US size J-10 (6.0 mm) crochet hook
  - Yarn needle
  - Pins

GAUGE
1 pattern repeat and 8 rows = 6 in./15 cm x 4 in./10 cm
Adjust hook size if necessary to obtain gauge.

NOTES
  - Similar #4 weight yarns may be substituted; please check gauge.
  - Beginning ch-1 does not count as a st.

INSTRUCTIONS

Ch 144 (160, 176, 192, 208).

Row 1 (RS): Sc in second ch from hook, *ch 1, skip 1 st, hdc in next, ch 1, skip 1 st, dc in next st, [ch 1, skip 1 st, tr in next] twice, ch 1, skip 1 st, dc in next st, ch 1, skip 1 st, hdc in next, ch 1, skip 1 st, sc in next*, ch 1, skip 1 st, sc in next; repeat from * across, ending last repeat at *, turn—9 (10, 11, 12, 13) pattern repeats.

Row 2: Ch 1, sc in each st and ch-1 space across, turn— 143 (159, 175, 191, 207) sc.

Row 3: Ch 5 (counts as tr, ch 1), *skip 1 sc, dc in next sc, ch 1, skip 1 sc, hdc in next sc, [ch 1, skip 1 sc, sc in next sc] twice, ch 1, skip 1 sc, hdc in next sc, ch 1, skip 1 sc, dc in next sc, ch 1, skip 1 sc, tr in next sc*, ch 1, skip 1 sc, tr in next; repeat from * across, ending last repeat at *, turn.

Row 4: Ch 1, sc in each st and ch-1 space across, turn— 143 (159, 175, 191, 207) sc.

Row 5: Ch 1, sc in first, *ch 1, skip 1 st, hdc in next, ch 1, skip 1 st, dc in next st, [ch 1, skip 1 st, tr in next] twice, ch 1, skip 1 st, dc in next st, ch 1, skip 1 st, hdc in next, ch 1, skip 1 st, sc in next*, ch 1, skip 1 st, sc in next; repeat from * across, ending last repeat at *, turn—9 (10, 11, 12, 13) pattern repeats.

Rows 6–40 (40, 44, 48, 50): Repeat *Rows 2–5*, ending on a repeat of *Row 2* or *Row 4*.

Fasten off.

Finishing

Block slightly before assembly. With WS facing, fold panel in 2 equal parts. Pin together. Beginning at side edge of Row 1, sew shoulder seam, leaving approximately 12.5 (12.5, 13, 13.5, 14) in./32 (32, 33, 34, 35.5) cm unsewn for neck opening. With RS facing, join yarn at seam with sl st and sc evenly around entire neckline. Fasten off and weave in ends.

Heartland Shrug

Designed by Ana Dyakova

The feminine look of this design will complement your everyday outfits. It is great to wear during the changing seasons or when you just want a little cover-up.

SKILL LEVEL
Intermediate

SIZES/FINISHED MEASUREMENTS
Small (Medium, Large, 1X, 2X)
Square Panel length/width: 39.5 (41.5, 43.5, 45.5, 47.5) in./100.5 (105.5, 110.5, 115.5, 120.5) cm
Armhole depth: 6.5 (6.5, 7, 7.5, 7.5) in./16.5 (16.5, 17.5, 19, 19) cm
Cuff height: 4.5 in./11.5 cm

YARN
Lion Brand Yarn Heartland, medium weight #4 yarn (100% acrylic; 251 yd./230 m per 5 oz./142g skein)
- 5 (5, 6, 7, 8) skeins Mammoth Cave 125

HOOK AND OTHER MATERIALS
- US size K-10½ (6.5 mm) crochet hook
- Yarn needle
- 2 stitch markers

GAUGE
12 dc and 6 rows = 4 in./10 cm
Adjust hook size if necessary to obtain gauge.

SPECIAL STITCHES
Beginning star (beginning star stitch). Ch 3, pull up loop in second ch from hook, in third ch from hook, in base of ch 3, and in next 2 sts (6 loops on hook), yo and pull through all 6 loops on hook, ch 1 (eye of star formed).
Star (star stitch). Pull up loop in eye of last star, in back of last loop of star, in same st as last leg of previous star, and in next 2 sts (6 loops on hook), yo and pull through all 6 loops on hook, ch 1.

NOTES
- Similar #4 weight yarns may be substituted; please check gauge.
- Pattern is worked in rows and then seamed together on the vertical sides to create armholes. Cuffs and star stitch edging are worked in rounds.

INSTRUCTIONS

Ch 99 (105, 111, 117, 123).

Row 1: Dc in third ch from hook and in each ch across, turn—96 (102, 108, 114, 120) dc.

Rows 2–63 (66, 69, 72, 75): Ch 3, dc in each st across, turn.

Fasten off. Fold piece in half so first st of each row meets last st of same row. *Count 20 (20, 22, 24, 24) dc rows up from fold and mark st for sleeve. Join yarn through first and last st of *Row 1*, and sl st through both layers across to marked st. Fasten off. On opposite side, first and last st of last rows should be aligned. Repeat from * for second sleeve.

Center Edging

Join yarn with sl st at center back at *Row 32 (33, 35, 37, 39)*.

Round 1 (RS): Ch 1, sc evenly around center opening, working 2 sc per row—252 (264, 276, 288, 300) sc.

Round 2: Beginning star, star st around, sl st to first st to join—126 (132, 138, 144, 150) star sts.

Round 3: Ch 1, 2 hdc in eye of each star st around, sl st to first hdc to join—252 (264, 276, 288, 300) hdc.

Rounds 4–9: Repeat *Rounds 2–3*.

Cuff

Join yarn with sl st at lower point of armhole on RS, where side seam begins.

Round 1: Beginning star, star st around, sl st to first st to join—20 (20, 22, 24, 24) star sts.

Round 2: Ch 1, 2 hdc in eye of each star st around, sl st to first hdc to join—40 (40, 44, 48, 48) hdc.

Rounds 3–8: Repeat *Rounds 1–2*.

Fasten off and weave in all ends.

Repeat Cuff instructions for second armhole.

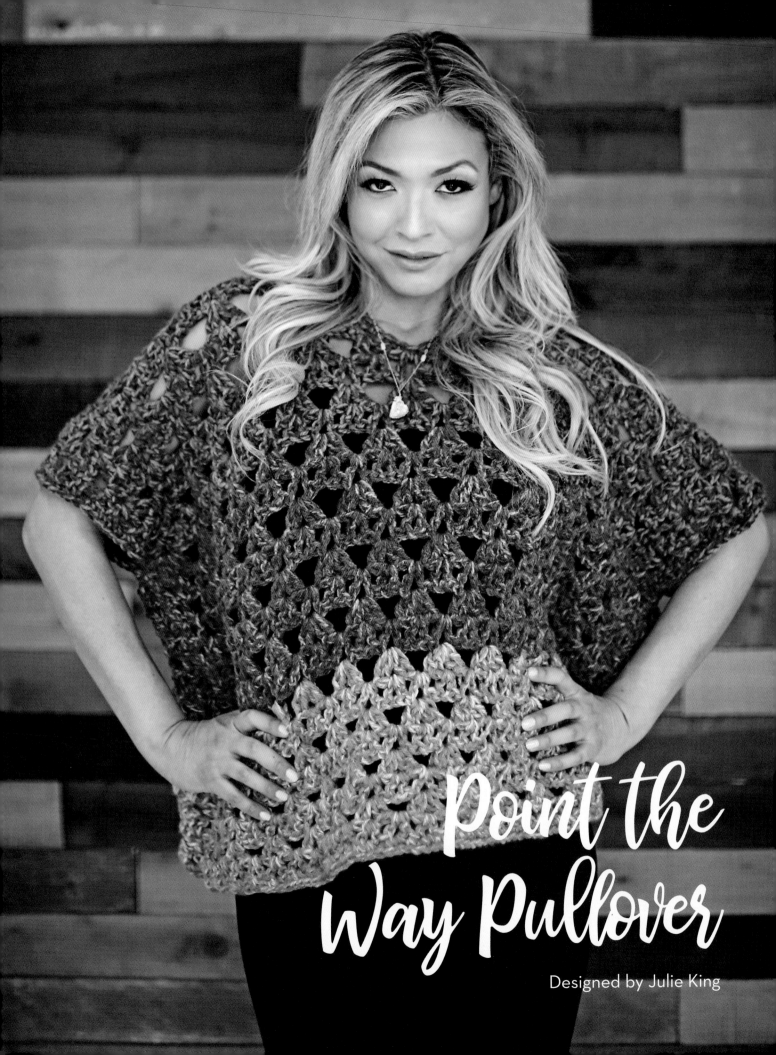

Point the Way Pullover

Designed by Julie King

This oversize top has a lot to offer: a slight V neck in the front, openwork design with peek-a-boo appeal, and chunky yarn for a style that looks and feels cozy!

SKILL LEVEL
Easy

SIZES/FINISHED MEASUREMENTS
Small (Medium, Large)
Width: 31 (36, 41) in./78.5 (91, 104) cm
Length: 19 (22, 25) in./48 (56, 63.5) cm

YARN
Lion Brand Yarn Wool-Ease Tonal, bulky weight #5 yarn
(80% acrylic, 20% wool; 124 yd./113 m per 4 oz./
113 g skein)
- 2 (2, 3) skeins Smoke 149 (Color A)
- 2 (2, 3) skeins Plum 145 (Color B)
- 2 (2, 3) skeins Charcoal 115 (Color C)

HOOK AND OTHER MATERIALS
- US size N-13 (9 mm) crochet hook
- Yarn needle
- 2 stitch markers

GAUGE
Ch 31 and work Rows 1–4 once. Resulting piece should
measure 4 in./10 cm tall, 12 in./30.5 cm wide.
Adjust hook size if necessary to obtain gauge.

SPECIAL STITCHES
V-st (V stitch). (Dc, ch 1, dc) in same st or ch-space.
Large v-st (large V stitch). [2 dc, ch 1, 2 dc] in same st
or ch-space.

NOTES
- Similar #5 weight yarns may be substituted; please
  check gauge.
- Pattern is worked in one piece starting at back
  waistline and ending at front waistline. Sides
  are then stitched together, and edging is added
  around the bottom, neckline, and armholes.
- Beginning ch-3 counts as first dc.
- Pattern is written for one solid color. Color
  changes for color block style are as follows:
  Small: Rows 1–7 (Color A), 8–14 (Color B), 15–27
  (Color C), 28–34 (Color B), 35–41 (Color A)

Medium: Rows 1–8 (Color A), 9–16 (Color B), 17–33 (Color C), 34–41 (Color B), 42–49 (Color A)

Large: Rows 1–9 (Color A), 10–18 (Color B), 19–39 (Color C), 40–48 (Color B), 49–57 (Color A)

INSTRUCTIONS

Beginning at Back Waistline

Ch 73 (85, 97).

Row 1: V-st in fifth ch from hook (skipped chs count as first dc), *skip 2 chs, v-st in next ch; repeat from * across to last 2 chs, skip 1 ch, dc in last, turn—23 (27, 31) v-sts, 2 dc.

Row 2 (RS): Ch 3, large v-st in ch-1 space of first v-st, *ch 1, skip 1 v-st, large v-st in ch-1 space of next v-st; repeat from * across, dc in last dc, turn—12 (14, 16) large v-sts, 2 dc.

Row 3: Ch 3, v-st in ch-1 space of first large v-st, v-st in next ch-1 space, *v-st in ch-1 space of next large v-st, v-st in next ch-1 space; repeat from * across, dc in last dc, turn—23 (27, 31) v-sts, 2 dc.

Row 4: Ch 3, dc in first dc of first v-st, ch 1, large v-st in ch-1 space of next v-st, *ch 1, skip 1 v-st, large v-st in ch-1 space of next v-st; repeat from * across to last v-st, ch 1, dc in last dc of last v-st, dc in last dc, turn—11 (13, 15) large v-sts, 4 dc.

Row 5: Ch 3, v-st in first ch-1 space, v-st in ch-1 space of next large v-st, *v-st in next ch-1 space, v-st in ch-1 space of next large v-st; repeat from * across, v-st in last ch-1 space, dc in last dc—23 (27, 31) v-sts, 2 dc.

Rows 6–21 (25, 29): Repeat *Rows 2–5,* 4 (5, 6) times. Leave yarn for Second Shoulder.

Split for Neckline

First Shoulder

Count 9 (11, 13) v-sts from beginning of row and place stitch marker in first dc of following v-st. Count 9 (11, 13) v-sts from end of row and place stitch marker in last dc of following v-st. The area between stitch markers forms the neck opening. Beginning on opposite side of last row, with RS facing, join yarn in marked st of *Row 21 (25, 29).*

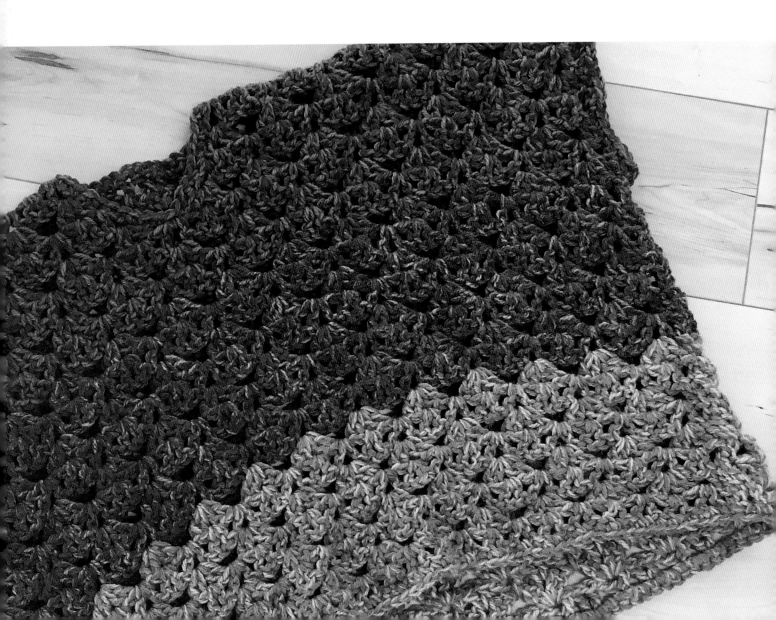

Row 22 (26, 30): Ch 3, large v-st in ch-1 space of first v-st, *ch 1, skip 1 v-st, large v-st in ch-1 space of next v-st; repeat from * 3 (4, 5) times, dc in last dc, turn—5 (6, 7) large v-sts, 2 dc.

Row 23 (27, 31): Ch 3, v-st in ch-1 space of first large v-st, v-st in next ch-1 space, *v-st in ch-1 space of next large v-st, v-st in next ch-1 space; repeat from * across, v-st in last dc, turn—9 (12, 13) v-sts, 1 dc.

Row 24 (28, 32): Ch 3, (dc, ch 1, 2 dc) in first v-st (counts as first large v-st), ch 1, skip 1 v-st, large v-st in ch-1 space of next v-st, *ch 1, skip 1 v-st, large v-st in ch-1 space of next v-st; repeat from * 2 (3, 4) times, ch 1, dc in last dc of last v-st, dc in last dc, turn—5 (6, 7) large v-sts, 2 dc.

Row 25 (29, 33): Ch 3, v-st in first ch-1 space, v-st in ch-1 space of first large v-st, *v-st in next ch-1 space, v-st in ch-1 space of next large v-st; repeat from * across, v-st in last dc of last large v-st—10 (13, 14) v-sts, 1 dc. Fasten off.

Second Shoulder

Pick up yarn at *Row 21 (25, 29)*.

Row 22 (26, 30): Ch 3, large v-st in ch-1 space of first v-st, *ch 1, skip 1 v-st, large v-st in ch-1 space of next v-st; repeat from * 3 (4, 5) times, dc in marked st, turn—5 (6, 7) large v-sts, 2 dc.

Row 23 (27, 31): Ch 4, dc in same st (counts as first v-st), v-st in ch-1 space of first large v-st, v-st in next ch-1 space, *v-st in ch-1 space of next large v-st, v-st in next ch-1 space; repeat from * across, dc in last dc, turn—9 (12, 13) v-sts, 1 dc.

Row 24 (28, 32): Ch 3, dc in first dc of first v-st, ch 1, large v-st in ch-1 space of next v-st, *ch 1, skip 1 v-st, large v-st in ch-1 space of next v-st; repeat from * across—5 (6, 7) large v-sts, 2 dc.

Row 25 (29, 33): Ch 4, dc in same st (counts as first v-st), v-st in ch-1 space of first large v-st, v-st in next ch-1 space, *v-st in ch-1 space of next large v-st, v-st in next ch-1 space; repeat from * across, dc in last dc, turn—10 (13, 14) v-sts, 1 dc.

Close Neckline

Row 26 (30, 34): Ch 3, large v-st in ch-1 space of first v-st, *ch 1, skip 1 v-st, large v-st in ch-1 space of next v-st*; repeat from * 4 (5, 6) times, ch 1, large v-st in ch-1 space of next v-st to close neckline; repeat from * to * 4 (5, 6) times, dc in last dc—12 (14, 16) large v-sts, 2 dc.

Rows 27 (31, 35)–29 (33, 37): Repeat *Rows 3–5* once.

Rows 30 (34, 38)–41 (49, 57): Repeat *Rows 2–5*, 3 (4, 5) times.

Fasten off.

Finishing

Block.

Side Seams

Fold piece in half along shoulder with RS facing in. With yarn needle, sew together both layers to seam side beginning at waistline and continuing for 12 (16, 20) rows. Fasten off and turn RS out.

Edging

With Color A, sc evenly around bottom edge. With Color C, sc evenly around Neckline and armholes. Fasten off and weave in all ends.

XOXO Kimono

Designed by Julie King

If you love to layer your look, especially in warmer weather, this piece is stunning! The openwork stitches make this a breezy style, and the abundant fringe makes a fun statement.

SKILL LEVEL
Easy

SIZES/FINISHED MEASUREMENTS
Small/Medium (Large/Extra Large)
Width: 35 (40) in./89 (101.5) cm
Length: 24 (30) in./61 (76) cm
Measurements do not include fringe.

YARN
Lion Brand Yarn 24/7 Cotton, medium weight #4 yarn
    (100% mercerized cotton; 186 yd./170 m per 3.5 oz./
    100 g skein)
  ▪ 6 (9) skeins Silver 149

HOOK AND OTHER MATERIALS
  ▪ US size I-9 (5.5 mm) crochet hook
  ▪ Yarn needle

GAUGE
4 crossed tr and 5 rows = 4 in./10 cm
Adjust hook size if necessary to obtain gauge.

SPECIAL STITCH
Crossed tr (crossed treble). Yo twice, insert hook in st,
    yo and pull up loop, yo and pull through 2 loops, yo,
    skip 2 sts and insert hook in st, yo and pull up loop,
    yo and pull through 2 loops (note: the two loops
    closest to the tip of hook will be referred to as center
    loops), [yo and pull through 2 loops] 3 times, ch 2, yo
    and insert hook in center loops, yo and pull through
    center loops, [yo and pull through 2 loops] twice.

NOTES
  ▪ Similar #4 weight yarns may be substituted; please
    check gauge.
  ▪ Pattern is worked in one piece in rows starting at
    the bottom of the Back and then split to work the
    Front sides. The two Front sides are folded in half
    and then stitched up to create armholes.
  ▪ Beginning ch-4 counts as first tr.

▮ INSTRUCTIONS

Back

Ch 145 (169).

Row 1: Crossed tr in fifth ch from hook (first 4 chs count as 1 tr), work 34 (40) crossed tr, tr in last ch, turn—35 (41) crossed tr, 2 tr.

Row 2: Ch 4 (counts as 1 tr), work 35 (41) crossed tr, tr in last st, turn—35 (41) crossed tr, 2 tr.

Rows 3–24 (30): Repeat *Row 2.*

Continue to Front.

Front

Row 1: Ch 4 (counts as 1 tr), work 14 (16) crossed tr, tr in first leg of next crossed tr, turn—14 (16) crossed tr, 2 tr.

Row 2: Ch 4 (counts as 1 tr), work 14 (16) crossed tr, tr in last st, turn—14 (16) crossed tr, 2 tr.

Rows 3–24 (30): Repeat *Row 2.*

Fasten off. Join yarn to opposite end of Row 24 (30) of Back and repeat Front instructions to create second side of Front.

Neckline Edging

Row 1: Join yarn to bottom corner, 4 sc around next 24 (30) tr, 4 sc in next 7 (9) crossed tr, 4 sc around next 24 (30) tr, turn—220 (276) sc.

Row 2: Ch 1 (not a st), sl st in each st, turn—220 (276) sl sts.

Row 3: Ch 1 (not a st), sc in each st, turn—220 (276) sc.

Row 4: Ch 1 (not a st), sl st in each st—220 (276) sl sts.

Finishing

Block to measurements.

Side Seams

Turn Kimono inside out. To create armholes, use a piece of yarn and yarn needle to stitch the Front to the Back. Start at bottom and stitch sides together, going up 12 (15) rows. Take care not to stitch too tightly. Fasten off and repeat for second side.

Fringe

Attach 4 pieces of fringe (16 in./40.5 cm long folded in half) to middle of each crossed tr around bottom of Kimono, to each tr around each armhole, and to each end of Neckline Edging.

Astrid Ruana

Designed by Toni Lipsey

This one-size-fits-most sleeveless sweater has incredible drape. Simple shapes and subtle striping are combined to make a cover-up that is perfect for any time of year!

SKILL LEVEL
Easy

SIZES/FINISHED MEASUREMENTS
One size fits most.
40 in./101.5 cm wide x 35 in./89 cm high

YARN
Lion Brand Yarn Vanna's Choice Solids, medium weight
  #4 yarn (100% acrylic; 170 yd./155 m per 3.5 oz./
  100 g ball)
- 5 balls Linen 099 (Color A)
- 3 balls Gray Marble 401 (Color B)

HOOK AND OTHER MATERIALS
- US size L-11 (8.0 mm) crochet hook
- Yarn needle

GAUGE
9 hdc and 7.5 rows = 4 in./10 cm
Adjust hook size if necessary to obtain gauge.

NOTES
- Similar #4 weight yarns may be substituted; please check gauge.
- Beginning ch-3 counts as first dc; beginning ch-2 counts as first hdc.

INSTRUCTIONS

First Panel

With Color A, ch 76.

Row 1: Hdc in third ch from hook and in each ch across to last ch, 2 dc in last, turn—76 sts.

Row 2: Ch 3, 2 dc in same, hdc in each st across, hdc in turning ch, turn—78 sts.

Row 3: Ch 2, skip 1 hdc, hdc in each st across to last st, 2 dc in last, 2 dc in turning ch, turn—80 sts.

Rows 4–37: Repeat *Rows 2 and 3* using the following color sequence: *Rows 4–22* Color A, *Rows 23–25* Color B, *Rows 26–29* Color A, *Rows 30–37* Color B—148 sts after last row.

Fasten off.

Second Panel

Row 1: Join Color A to base of beginning ch-2 of First Panel Row 1, ch 2, hdc in each remaining loop of beginning ch across to last, 2 dc in last, turn—76 sts.

Rows 2–37: Work as for First Panel. Continue to Finishing.

Finishing

Fold First Panel in half so first st of Row 37 aligns with last st of Row 37. Repeat fold for Second Panel. Seam both Panels as follows: Join Color B through WS of both layers of Row 37, ch 1, sc through both layers across, leaving 7 in./17.5 cm open for armholes. Fasten off and weave in ends. Hang garment and steam block.

Stonewashed Shrug

Designed by Jess Mason

This easy shrug pattern will have you wrapped up in style in no time! The drape falls just right, making this piece a stylish accessory with so much wardrobe potential.

SKILL LEVEL
Easy

SIZES/FINISHED MEASUREMENTS
One size
Width: 54 in./137 cm
Height: 30 in./76 cm

YARN
Lion Brand Yarn Jeans, medium weight #4 yarn (100% acrylic; 246 yd./225 m per 3.5 oz./100 g skein)
- 5 skeins Stonewash 109

HOOK AND OTHER MATERIALS
- US size I-9 (5.5 mm) crochet hook
- Yarn needle

GAUGE
16 sts and 6 rows = 4 in./10 cm
Adjust hook size if necessary to obtain gauge.

SPECIAL STITCH
Hdc2tog (half double crochet 2 stitches together).
Yo and insert hook in next st, yo and pull up loop, yo and pull through 1 loop on hook (3 loops on hook), insert hook in next st, yo and pull up loop, yo and pull through 1 loop on hook, (4 loops on hook) yo and pull through all loops on hook.

NOTES
- Similar #4 weight yarns may be substituted; please check gauge.
- Beginning ch-4 counts as (dc, ch-1).
- Beginning ch-3 counts as first dc.

INSTRUCTIONS

Ch 122.

Row 1: Dc in second ch from hook, *ch 1, skip 1, dc in next; repeat from * across, turn—119 sts.

Row 2: Ch 4, skip 1 dc and ch-1 space, *dc in next dc, ch 1, skip 1; repeat from * across, turn—119 sts.

Rows 3–5: Repeat *Row 2.*

Row 6: Ch 3, *hdc2tog over ch-1 space and next dc, ch 1; repeat from * across to turning ch, dc in turning ch, turn—118 sts.

Row 7: Ch 3, *hdc2tog over ch-1 space and hdc2tog, ch 1; repeat from * across to turning ch, hdc in top of turning ch, turn—118 sts.

Row 8: Ch 4, *dc in next, ch 1, skip 1; repeat from * across, dc in turning ch, turn—119 sts.

Rows 9–12: Repeat *Row 2.*

Repeat *Rows 6–12* until piece measures approximately 54 in./137 cm long, ending on a repeat of *Row 12.* Fasten off.

Finishing

Fold fabric in half lengthwise so first st of Row 1 meets last st of Row 1. Join yarn through WS of both layers at Row 1, sc evenly across to seam for 12 in./30.5 cm. Fasten off. Join yarn to opposite end through WS of both layers of last row, sc evenly across for 12 in./30.5 cm. Fasten off. With RS facing, join yarn to any st in remaining center opening, ch 1, sc evenly around opening, sl st to join. Repeat sc edging for each armhole. Fasten off and weave in all ends.

Inverted Triangles Shrug

Designed by Amber Millard

Give this cozy, simple, and surprisingly quick shrug a try. The cocoon shape and creative colorwork will make a design you'll have a hard time taking off!

SKILL LEVEL
Experienced

SIZES/FINISHED MEASUREMENTS
Small (Medium, Large, 1X, 2X)
Width: 29.5 (34, 38.5, 43, 47.5) in./75 (86.5, 98, 109, 120.5) cm
Height: 30 (35, 40, 45, 50) in./76 (89, 101.5, 114, 127) cm

YARN
Lion Brand Yarn New Basic 175, medium weight #4 yarn (75% acrylic, 25% wool; 175 yd./160 m per 3.5 oz./100 g skein)
- 2 (3, 3, 4, 6) skeins Ice 106 (Color A)
- 1 (1, 2, 2, 2) skeins Camel 124 (Color B)
- 1 (1, 2, 2, 2) skeins Petrol Blue 109 (Color C)
- 1 skein Pumpkin 133 (Color D)
- 1 skein Mango 132 (Color E)
- 1 skein Wisteria 144 (Color F)
- 1 skein Turquoise 148 (Color G)

HOOK AND OTHER MATERIALS
- US size I-9 (5.5 mm) crochet hook
- Measuring tape
- Yarn needle

GAUGE
14 dc and 7 rows = 4 in./10 cm
Adjust hook size if necessary to obtain gauge.

NOTES
- The ch-3 at the beginning of each row counts as first dc.
- This pattern is worked in two parts: the main body, which is worked back and forth in rows, and the finishing, which is worked in the round after seaming to create the armholes.
- Every stitch in this pattern is a double crochet. Pattern instructs what color to use (Color A, Color B, etc.), and the number in parentheses tells how many dc to work in that color.
- Begin each row with a ch-3 and turn after each row.

- When changing colors, drop old color and pick up new color. Do not carry colors. Use two skeins of Color B and work from each side.
- All size designs are similar but not exactly the same. (Medium is modeled.)

INSTRUCTIONS

Small Body

With Color A, ch 108.

Row 1: Dc in fourth ch from hook and in each ch across, turn—105 dc here and throughout.

Ch 3 (counts as first dc) to begin each row, turn to end each row for remainder of pattern.

Rows 2–3: Ch 3, dc in next 104, turn.

Rows 4–6: Color B ch 3, (6), Color A (91), Color B (7).

Rows 7–8: Color B ch 3, (13), Color A (77), Color B (14). Fasten off Color A.

Rows 9–11: Color B ch 3, (20), Color C (63), Color B (21).

Rows 12–14: Color B ch 3, (27), Color C (49), Color B (28).

Rows 15–16: Color B ch 3, (34), Color C (35), Color B (35). Fasten off Color C.

Rows 17–19: Color B ch 3, (41), Color D (21), Color B (42).

Rows 20–21: Color B ch 3, (48), Color D (7), Color B (49). Fasten off Color D.

Rows 22–25: Color B ch 3, (104).

Rows 26–27: Color B ch 3, (48), Color E (7), Color B (49).

Rows 28–30: Color B ch 3, (41), Color E (21), Color B (42). Fasten off Color E.

Rows 31–32: Color B ch 3, (34), Color F (35), Color B (35).

Rows 33–35: Color B ch 3, (27), Color F (49), Color B (28).

Rows 36–38: Color B ch 3, (20), Color F (63), Color B (21). Fasten off Color F.

Rows 39–40: Color B ch 3, (13), Color G (77), Color B (14).

Rows 41–43: Color B ch 3, (6), Color G (91), Color B (7). Fasten off Color B.

Rows 44–46: Color G ch 3, (104). Fasten off Color G.

Fold piece in half lengthwise so *Row 1* meets *Row 46*. With yarn needle, sew together row ends of *Rows 1–7* to last 7 rows. Repeat for second size. This leaves two armholes and a center opening.

Medium Body

With Color A, ch 123.

Row 1: Dc in fourth ch from hook and in each ch across, turn—120 dc here and throughout.

Ch 3 (counts as first dc) to begin each row, turn to end each row for remainder of pattern.

Rows 2–3: Ch 3, dc in next 119, turn.

Rows 4–6: Color B ch 3, (7), Color A (104), Color B (8).

Rows 7–9: Color B ch 3, (15), Color A (88), Color B (16). Fasten off Color A.

Rows 10–12: Color B ch 3, (23), Color C (72), Color B (24).

Rows 13–15: Color B ch 3, (31), Color C (56), Color B (32).

Rows 16–18: Color B ch 3, (39), Color C (40), Color B (40). Fasten off Color C.

Rows 19–21: Color B ch 3, (47), Color D (24), Color B (48).

Rows 22–24: Color B ch 3, (55), Color D (8), Color B (56). Fasten off Color D.

Rows 25–28: Color B ch 3, (119).

Rows 29–31: Color B ch 3, (55), Color E (8), Color B (56).

Rows 32–34: Color B ch 3, (47), Color E (24), Color B (48). Fasten off Color E.

Rows 35–37: Color B ch 3, (39), Color F (40), Color B (40).

Rows 38–40: Color B ch 3, (31), Color F (56), Color B (32).

Rows 41–43: Color B ch 3, (23), Color F (72), Color B (24). Fasten off Color F.

Rows 44–46: Color B ch 3, (15), Color G (88), Color B (16).

Rows 47–49: Color B ch 3, (7), Color G (104), Color B (8). Fasten off Color B.

Rows 50–52: Color G ch 3, (119). Fasten off Color G.

Fold piece in half lengthwise so *Row 1* meets *Row 52*. With yarn needle, sew together row ends of *Rows 1–10* to last 10 rows. Repeat for second size. This leaves two armholes and a center opening.

Large Body

With Color A, ch 138.

Row 1: Dc in fourth ch from hook and in each ch across, turn—135 dc here and throughout.

Ch 3 (counts as first dc) to begin each row, turn to end each row for remainder of pattern.

Rows 2–4: Ch 3, dc in next 134, turn.

Rows 5–7: Color B ch 3, (8), Color A (117), Color B (9).

Rows 8–10: Color B ch 3, (17), Color A (99), Color B (18). Fasten off Color A.

Rows 11–14: Color B ch 3, (26), Color C (81), Color B (27).

Rows 15–17: Color B ch 3, (35), Color C (63), Color B (36).

Rows 18–20: Color B ch 3, (44), Color C (45), Color B (45). Fasten off Color C.

Rows 21–24: Color B ch 3, (53), Color D (27), Color B (54).

Rows 25–27: Color B ch 3, (62), Color D (9), Color B (63). Fasten off Color D.

Rows 28–31: Color B ch 3, (134).

Rows 32–34: Color B ch 3, (62), Color E (9), Color B (63).

Rows 35–38: Color B ch 3, (53), Color E (27), Color B (54). Fasten off Color E.

Rows 39–41: Color B ch 3, (44), Color F (45), Color B (45).

Rows 42–44: Color B ch 3, (35), Color F (63), Color B (36).

Rows 45–48: Color B ch 3, (26), Color F (81), Color B (27). Fasten off Color F.

Rows 49–51: Color B ch 3, (17), Color G (99), Color B (18).

Rows 52–54: Color B ch 3, (8), Color G (117), Color B (9). Fasten off Color B.

Rows 55–58: Color G ch 3, (134). Fasten off Color G.

Fold piece in half lengthwise so *Row 1* meets *Row 58*. With yarn needle, sew together row ends of *Rows 1–11* to last 11 rows. Repeat for second size. This leaves two armholes and a center opening.

1X Body

With Color A, ch 153.

Row 1: Dc in fourth ch from hook and in each ch across, turn—150 dc here and throughout.

Ch 3 (counts as first dc) to begin each row, turn to end each row for remainder of pattern.

Rows 2–5: Ch 3, dc in next 149, turn.

Rows 6–9: Color B ch 3, (9), Color A (130), Color B (10).

Rows 10–12: Color B ch 3, (19), Color A (110), Color B (20). Fasten off Color A.

Rows 13–17: Color B ch 3, (29), Color C (90), Color B (30).

Rows 18–21: Color B ch 3, (39), Color C (70), Color B (40).

Rows 22–24: Color B ch 3, (49), Color C (50), Color B (50). Fasten off Color C.

Rows 25–28: Color B ch 3, (59), Color D (30), Color B (60).

Rows 29–31: Color B ch 3, (69), Color D (10), Color B (70). Fasten off Color D.

Rows 32–35: Color B ch 3, (149).

Rows 36–38: Color B ch 3, (69), Color E (10), Color B (70).

Rows 39–42: Color B ch 3, (59), Color E (30), Color B (60). Fasten off Color E.

Rows 43–45: Color B ch 3, (49), Color F (50), Color B (50).

Rows 46–49: Color B ch 3, (39), Color F (70), Color B (40).

Rows 50–54: Color B ch 3, (29), Color F (90), Color B (30). Fasten off Color F.

Rows 55–57: Color B ch 3, (19), Color G (110), Color B (20).

Rows 58–61: Color B ch 3, (9), Color G (130), Color B (10). Fasten off Color B.

Rows 62–66: Color G ch 3, (149). Fasten off Color G.

Fold piece in half lengthwise so *Row 1* meets *Row 66*. With yarn needle, sew together row ends of *Rows 1–15* to last 15 rows. Repeat for second size. This leaves two armholes and a center opening.

2X Body

With Color A, ch 168.

Row 1: Dc in fourth ch from hook and in each ch across, turn—165 dc here and throughout.

Ch 3 (counts as first dc) to begin each row, turn to end each row for remainder of pattern.

Rows 2–5: Ch 3, dc in next 164, turn.

Rows 6–9: Color B ch 3, (10), Color A (143), Color B (11).

Rows 10–13: Color B ch 3, (21), Color A (121), Color B (22). Fasten off Color A.

Rows 14–18: Color B ch 3, (32), Color C (99), Color B (33).

Rows 19–22: Color B ch 3, (43), Color C (77), Color B (44).

Rows 23–26: Color B ch 3, (54), Color C (55), Color B (55). Fasten off Color C.

Rows 27–31: Color B ch 3, (65), Color D (33), Color B (66).

Rows 32–35: Color B ch 3, (76), Color D (11), Color B (77). Fasten off Color D.

Rows 36–39: Color B ch 3, (164).

Rows 40–43: Color B ch 3, (76), Color E (11), Color B (77).

Rows 44–48: Color B ch 3, (65), Color E (33), Color B (66). Fasten off Color E.

Rows 49–52: Color B ch 3, (54), Color F (55), Color B (55).

Rows 53–56: Color B ch 3, (43), Color F (77), Color B (44).

Rows 57–61: Color B ch 3, (32), Color F (99), Color B (33). Fasten off Color F.

Rows 62–65: Color B ch 3, (21), Color G (121), Color B (22).

Rows 66–69: Color B ch 3, (10), Color G (143), Color B (11). Fasten off Color B.

Rows 70–74: Color G ch 3, (164). Fasten off Color G.

Fold piece in half lengthwise so *Row 1* meets *Row 74*. With yarn needle, sew together row ends of *Rows 1–20* to last 20 rows. Repeat for second size. This leaves two armholes and a center opening.

Finishing

Join Color A to first st of Color A section.

Round 1: Ch 3, dc in each st across to next color, with Color G, dc in each remaining st, sl st to first dc to join, turn.

Round 2: Ch 3, dc in each st of color section, with Color A, dc in each remaining st, sl st to third ch of beginning ch-3 to join, turn.

Round 3: With Color A, ch 3, dc in each st of color section, with Color G, dc in each remaining st, sl st to third ch of beginning ch-3 to join.

Fasten off and weave in all ends.

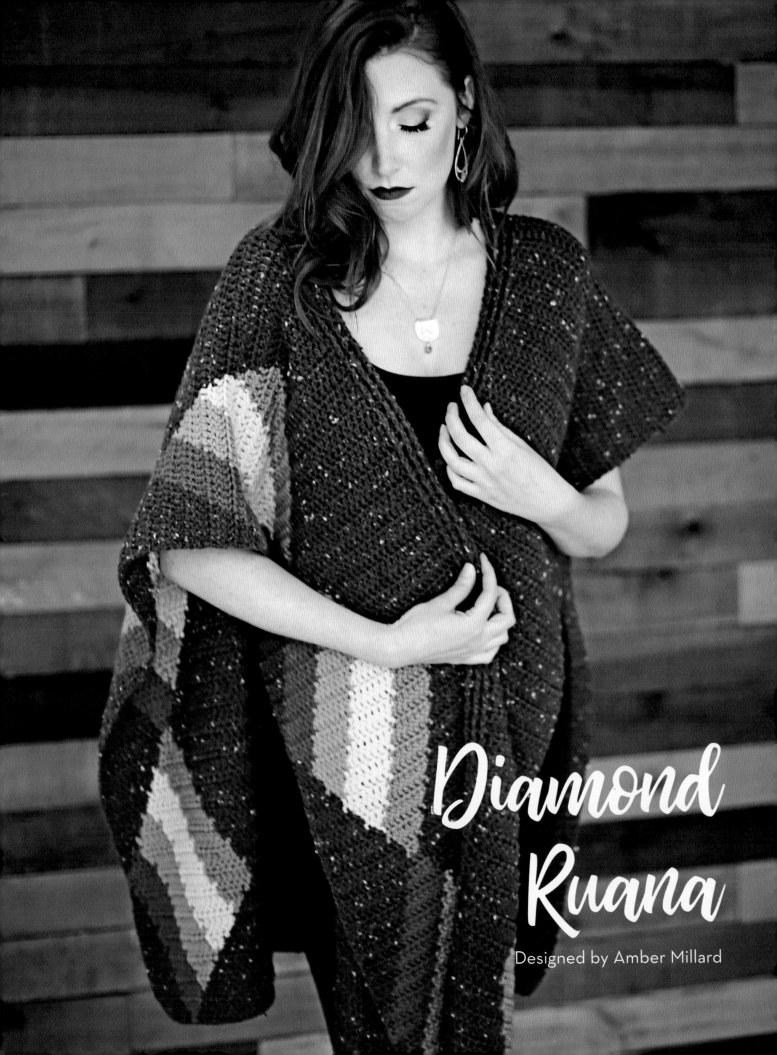

Diamond Ruana

Designed by Amber Millard

Cozy, warm, and so fun—this ruana design is a big one but very rewarding when you finish it. You'll feel a sense of pride when you're curled up with a good book in this squishy and warm ruana!

SKILL LEVEL
Experienced

SIZES/FINISHED MEASUREMENTS
One size fits most.
Back panel: 37 in./94 cm width x 44 in./112 cm height (front panels each measure 44 in./112 cm long; garment total length = 88 in./223.5 cm)

YARN
Lion Brand Yarn Vanna's Choice, medium weight #4 yarn (100% acrylic; 170 yd./155 m per 3.5 oz./100 g skein)
- 11 skeins Graphite 407 (Color A)
- 1 skein Olive 174 (Color B)
- 1 skein Dusty Green 173 (Color C)
- 1 skein Silver Blue 105 (Color D)
- 1 skein Silver Grey 149 (Color E)

HOOK AND OTHER MATERIALS
- US size I-9 (5.5 mm) crochet hook
- Yarn needle

GAUGE
14 dc and 7 rows = 4 in./10 cm
Adjust hook size if necessary to obtain gauge.

NOTES
- Similar #4 weight yarns may be substituted; please check gauge.
- The ch-3 at the beginning of each row counts as first dc. Begin each row with a ch-3 and turn after each row.
- Pattern is worked in three parts: Back and two Front Panels.
- Every stitch in this pattern is a double crochet. Pattern instructs what color to use (A, B, etc.), and the number in parentheses tells how many dc to work in that color.
- Chart shown on page 61 illustrates the diamond pattern.

INSTRUCTIONS

Back

Row 1: With A, ch 130, dc into the fourth ch from the hook (the skipped sts count as a dc) and into the next 13 sts; cont with B (2) and A (111)—128 dc here and throughout section.

Row 2: With A, ch 3, (109), B (4), A (14).

Row 3: With A, ch 3, (12), B (6), A (109).

Row 4: With A, ch 3, (107), B (8), A (12).

Row 5: With A, ch 3, (10), B (8), C (2), A (107).

Row 6: With A, ch 3, (105), C (4), B (8), A (10).

Row 7: With A, ch 3, (8), B (8), C (6), A (105).

Row 8: With A, ch 3, (103), C (8), B (8), A (8).

Row 9: With A, ch 3, (6), B (8), C (8), D (2), A (103).

Row 10: With A, ch 3, (101), D (4), C (8), B (8), A (6).

Row 11: With A, ch 3, (4), B (8), C (8), D (6), A (101).

Row 12: With A, ch 3, (99), D (8), C (8), B (8), A (4).

Row 13: With A, ch 3, (2), B (8), C (8), D (8), E (2), A (99).

Row 14: With A, ch 3, (97), E (4), D (8), C (8), B (8), A (2).

Row 15: With A, ch 3, B (8), C (8), D (8), D (6), A (97).

Row 16: With A, ch 3, (95), E (8), D (8), C (8), B (8).

Row 17: With A, ch 3, B (6), C (8), D (8), E (8), A (97).

Row 18: With A, ch 3, (97), E (8), D (8), C (8), B (4), A (2).

Row 19: With A, ch 3, (2), B (2), C (8), D (8), E (8), A (99).

Fasten off Color B.

Row 20: With A, ch 3, (99), E (8), D (8), C (8), A (4).

Row 21: With A, ch 3, (4), C (6), D (8), E (8), A (101).

Row 22: With A, ch 3, (101), E (8), D (8), C (4), A (6).

Row 23: With A, ch 3, (6), C (2), D (8), E (8), A (103).

Fasten off Color C.

Row 24: With A, ch 3, (103), E (8), D (8), A (8).

Row 25: With A, ch 3, (8), D (6), E (8), A (105).

Row 26: With A, ch 3, (105), E (8), D (4), A (10).

Row 27: With A, ch 3, (10), D (2), E (8), A (107).

Fasten off Color D.

Row 28: With A, ch 3, (107), E (8), A (12).

Row 29: With A, ch 3, (12), E (6), A (109).

Row 30: With A, ch 3, (109), E (4), A (14).

Row 31: With A, ch 3, (14), E (2), A (111).

Fasten off Color E.

Row 32: With A, ch 3, (110), B (2), A (15).

Row 33: With A, ch 3, (13), B (4), A (110).

Row 34: With A, ch 3, (108), B (6), A (13).

Row 35: With A, ch 3, (11), B (8), A (108).

Row 36: With A, ch 3, (106), C (2), B (8), A (11).

Row 37: With A, ch 3, (9), B (8), C (4), A (106).

Row 38: With A, ch 3, (104), C (6), B (8), A (9).

Row 39: With A, ch 3, (7), B (8), C (8), A (104).

Row 40: With A, ch 3, (102), D (2), C (8), B (8), A (7).

Row 41: With A, ch 3, (5), B (8), C (8), D (4), A (102).

Row 42: With A, ch 3, (100), D (6), C (8), B (8), A (5).

Row 43: With A, ch 3, (3), B (8), C (8), D (8), A (100).

Row 44: With A, ch 3, (98), E (2), D (8), C (8), B (8), A (3).

Row 45: With A, ch 3, (1), B (8), C (8), D (8), E (4), A (98).

Row 46: With A, ch 3, (96), E (6), D (8), C (8), B (8), A (1).

Row 47: With B, ch 3, (7), C (8), D (8), E (8), A (96).

Row 48: With A, ch 3, (96), E (8), D (8), C (8), B (6), A (1).

Row 49: With A, ch 3, (1), B (4), C (8), D (8), E (8), A (98).

Row 50: With A, ch 3, (98), E (8), D (8), C (8), B (2), A (3).

Fasten off Color B.

Row 51: With A, ch 3, (3), C (8), D (8), E (8), A (100).

Row 52: With A, ch 3, (100), E (8), D (8), C (6), A (5).

Row 53: With A, ch 3, (5), C (4), D (8), E (8), A (102).

Row 54: With A, ch 3, (102), E (8), D (8), C (2), A (7).

Fasten off Color C.

Row 55: With A, ch 3, (7), D (8), E (8), A (104).

Row 56: With A, ch 3, (104), E (8), D (6), A (9).

Row 57: With A, ch 3, (9), D (4), E (8), A (106).

Row 58: With A, ch 3, (106), E (8), D (2), A (11).

Fasten off Color D.

Row 59: With A, ch 3, (11), E (8), A (108).

Row 60: With A, ch 3, (108), E (6), A (13).

Row 61: With A, ch 3, (13), E (4), A (110).

Row 62: With A, ch 3, (110), E (2), A (15).

Fasten off Color E.

Row 63: With A, ch 3, (14), B (2), A (111).

Row 64: With A, ch 3, (109), B (4), A (14).

Row 65: With A, ch 3, (12), B (6), A (109).

Row 66: With A, ch 3, (107), B (8), A (12).

Row 67: With A, ch 3, (10), B (8), C (2), A (107).

Row 68: With A, ch 3, (105), C (4), B (8), A (10).

Row 69: With A, ch 3, (8), B (8), C (6), A (105).

Row 70: With A, ch 3, (103), C (8), B (8), A (8).

Row 71: With A, ch 3, (6), B (8), C (8), D (2), A (103).

Row 72: With A, ch 3, (101), D (4), C (8), B (8), A (6).

Row 73: With A, ch 3, (4), B (8), C (8), D (6), A (101).

Row 74: With A, ch 3, (99), D (8), C (8), B (8), A (4).

Row 75: With A, ch 3, (2), B (8), C (8), D (8), E (2), A (99).

Row 76: With A, ch 3, (97), E (4), D (8), C (8), B (8), A (2).

Row 77: With A, ch 3, B (8), C (8), D (8), D (6), A (97).

Row 78: With A, ch 3, (95), E (8), D (8), C (8), B (8).

Continue to First Front Panel.

First Front Panel

This section forms a post stitch border along the front opening. Odd-numbered rows always end the same, and even-numbered rows begin the same. Add the following instructions to each row:

Last 6 sts of odd rows: With A [fpdc around next, bpdc around next] twice, fpdc in next, dc in turning ch, turn.

First 6 sts of even rows: With A, ch 3, [bpdc around next, fpdc around next] twice, bpdc around next . . .

Continuing from *Row 78* of Back:

Row 1: With A, ch 3, B (6), C (8), D (8), E (8), A (14)—51 dc here and throughout section.

Row 2: With A (15), E (8), D (8), C (8), B (4), A (2).

Row 3: With A, ch 3, (2), B (2), C (8), D (8), E (8), A (16).

Fasten off Color B.

Row 4: With A (17), E (8), D (8), C (8), A (4).

Row 5: With A, ch 3, (4), C (6), D (8), E (8), A (18).

Row 6: With A (19), E (8), D (8), C (4), A (6).

Row 7: With A, ch 3, (6), C (2), D (8), E (8), A (20). Fasten off Color C.

Row 8: With A (21), E (8), D (8), A (8).

Row 9: With A, ch 3, (8), D (6), E (8), A (22).

Row 10: With A (23), E (8), D (4), A (10).

Row 11: With A, ch 3, (10), D (2), E (8), A (24). Fasten off Color D.

Row 12: With A (25), E (8), A (12).

Row 13: With A, ch 3, (12), E (6), A (26).

Row 14: With A (27), E (4), A (14).

Row 15: With A, ch 3, (14), E (2), A (28). Fasten off Color E.

Row 16: With A (28), B (2), A (15).

Row 17: With A, ch 3, (13), B (4), A (27).

Row 18: With A (26), B (6), A (13).

Row 19: With A, ch 3, (11), B (8), A (25).

Row 20: With A (24), C (2), B (8), A (11).

Row 21: With A, ch 3, (9), B (8), C (4), A (23).

Row 22: With A (22), C (6), B (8), A (9).

Row 23: With A, ch 3, (7), B (8), C (8), A (21).

Row 24: With A (20), D (2), C (8), B (8), A (7).

Row 25: With A, ch 3, (5), B (8), C (8), D (4), A (19).

Row 26: With A (18), D (6), C (8), B (8), A (5).

Row 27: With A, ch 3, (3), B (8), C (8), D (8), A (17).

Row 28: With A (16), E (2), D (8), C (8), B (8), A (3).

Row 29: With A, ch 3, (1), B (8), C (8), D (8), E (4), A (15).

Row 30: With A (14), E (6), D (8), C (8), B (8), A (1).

Row 31: With B, ch 3, (7), C (8), D (8), E (8), A (13).

Row 32: With A (14), E (8), D (8), C (8), B (6), A (1).

Row 33: With A, ch 3, (1), B (4), C (8), D (8), E (8), A (15).

Row 34: With A (16), E (8), D (8), C (8), B (2), A (3). Fasten off Color B.

Row 35: With A, ch 3, (3), C (8), D (8), E (8), A (17).

Row 36: With A (18), E (8), D (8), C (6), A (5).

Row 37: With A, ch 3, (5), C (4), D (8), E (8), A (19).
Row 38: With A (20), E (8), D (8), C (2), A (7). Fasten off Color C.
Row 39: With A, ch 3, (7), D (8), E (8), A (21).
Row 40: With A (22), E (8), D (6), A (9).
Row 41: With A, ch 3, (9), D (4), E (8), A (23).
Row 42: With A (24), E (8), D (2), A (11). Fasten off Color D.
Row 43: With A, ch 3, (11), E (8), A (25).
Row 44: With A (26), E (6), A (13).
Row 45: With A, ch 3, (13), E (4), A (27).
Row 46: With A (28), E (2), A (15). Fasten off Color E.
Row 47: With A, ch 3, (14), B (2), A (28).
Row 48: With A (27), B (4), A (14).
Row 49: With A, ch 3, (12), B (6), A (26).
Row 50: With A (25), B (8), A (12).
Row 51: With A, ch 3, (10), B (8), C (2), A (24).
Row 52: With A (23), C (4), B (8), A (10).
Row 53: With A, ch 3, (8), B (8), C (6), A (22).
Row 54: With A (21), C (8), B (8), A (8).
Row 55: With A, ch 3, (6), B (8), C (8), D (2), A (20).
Row 56: With A (19), D (4), C (8), B (8), A (6).
Row 57: With A, ch 3, (4), B (8), C (8), D (6), A (18).
Row 58: With A (17), D (8), C (8), B (8), A (4).
Row 59: With A, ch 3, (2), B (8), C (8), D (8), E (2), A (16).
Row 60: With A (15), E (4), D (8), C (8), B (8), A (2).
Row 61: With A, ch 3, B (8), C (8), D (8), E (6), A (14).
Row 62: With A (13), E (8), D (8), C (8), B (8).
Row 63: With A, ch 3, B (6), C (8), D (8), E (8), A (14).
Row 64: With A (15), E (8), D (8), C (8), B (4), A (2).
Row 65: With A, ch 3, (2), B (2), C (8), D (8), E (8), A (16). Fasten off Color B.
Row 66: With A (17), E (8), D (8), C (8), A (4).
Row 67: With A, ch 3, (4), C (6), D (8), E (8), A (18).
Row 68: With A (19), E (8), D (8), C (4), A (6).
Row 69: With A, ch 3, (6), C (2), D (8), E (8), A (20). Fasten off Color C.
Row 70: With A (21), E (8), D (8), A (8).
Row 71: With A, ch 3, (8), D (6), E (8), A (22).
Row 72: With A (23), E (8), D (4), A (10).
Row 73: With A, ch 3, (10), D (2), E (8), A (24). Fasten off Color D.
Row 74: With A (25), E (8), A (12).
Row 75: With A, ch 3, (12), E (6), A (26).
Row 76: With A (27), E (4), A (14).
Row 77: With A, ch 3, (14), E (2), A (28).
Fasten off Colors A and E. Weave in all ends.

Second Front Panel

Begin in last st of *Row 78*. (The skipped stitches in the middle are the space for the neck.)
Row 1: With A, ch 3, dc in next 44 sts, [bpdc around next, fpdc around next] twice, bpdc around next, dc in last, turn.
Row 2: With A, ch 3, [bpdc around next, fpdc around next] twice, bpdc around next, dc in next 45 sts.
Rows 3–77: Repeat *Rows 1–2*.
Fasten off and weave in ends.

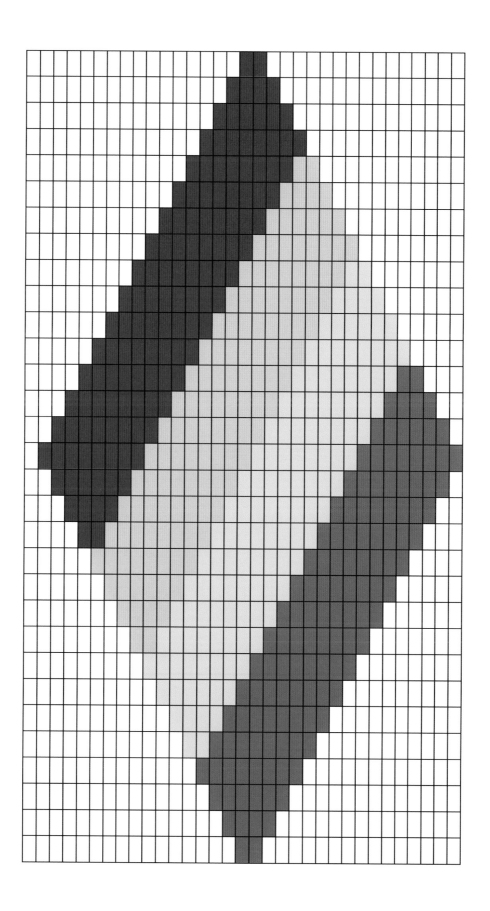

Penning Poncho

Designed by
Katy Petersen

This cozy and oversize layering garment is a staple for any wardrobe! This poncho style is perfect for beginners, too, because it uses basic stitches and has no seams.

SKILL LEVEL
Easy

SIZES/FINISHED MEASUREMENTS
Small/Medium (Large/1X, 2X/3X)
Width: 32 (34, 36) in./81 (86.5, 91) cm
Front height: 26 (27, 28) in./66 (68.5, 71) cm
Back height: 28 (29, 30) in./71 (73.5, 76) cm
To fit shoulder width: 14–15 (16–17, 18–19) in./35.5–38 (40.5–43, 45.5–48) cm

YARN
Lion Brand Yarn Wool-Ease, medium weight #4 yarn (80% acrylic, 20% wool; 197 yd./180 m per 3 oz./85 g skein)
- 9 (9, 10) skeins Natural Heather 98

HOOK AND OTHER MATERIALS
- US size H-8 (5.0 mm) crochet hook
- 2 size-4 snaps (optional)
- Yarn needle

GAUGE
18 sts in pattern and 11 rows = 4 in./10 cm square (blocked)
Adjust hook size if necessary to obtain gauge.

NOTES
- Similar #4 weight yarns may be substituted; please check gauge.
- Poncho is worked in one piece. The Front Trim is worked first, then the Front, the Split for Neck opening, the Back, and finally the Back Trim and Side Trims.

INSTRUCTIONS

Front Trim

Ch 10.

Row 1: Sc in second ch from hook and in each ch across, turn—9 sc.

Row 2: Ch 1, BLO sc in each st across.

Repeat *Row 2* until 140 (148, 156) rows complete.

Front

Rotate piece to work into row ends.

Row 1 (WS): Ch 1 (does not count as a st here and throughout), sc in each trim row end, turn—140 (148, 156) sc.

Work in FLO for remainder of section.

Row 2 (RS): Ch 2, dc in first 44 (48, 52), [sc in next, dc in next] 26 times, dc in last 44 (48, 52) sts, turn—140 (148, 156) sts.

Row 3: Ch 1, sc in first 44 (48, 52), [sc in next, dc in next] 26 times, sc in last 44 (48, 52) sts, turn—140 (148, 156) sts.

Repeat *Rows 2 and 3* until 58 (60, 64) rows complete, ending on a repeat of *Row 2*.

Continue to next section without fastening off.

Split for Neck

First Side

Work in FLO for this section.

Row 1: Ch 1, sc in first 44 (48, 52), [sc in next, dc in next] 4 times, turn—52 (56, 60) sts.

Row 2: Ch 1, [sc in next, dc in next] 4 times, dc in last 44 (48, 52) sts, turn—52 (56, 60) sts.

Repeat *Rows 1 and 2* until 9 rows complete, ending on a repeat of *Row 1*.

Fasten off.

Second Side

Skip 36 sts from First Side and join yarn.

Work in FLO for this section.

Row 1: Ch 1, [sc in next, dc in next] 4 times, sc in last 44 (48, 52), turn—52 (56, 60) sts.

Row 2: Ch 2, dc in next 44 (48, 52), [sc in next, dc in next] 4 times, turn—52 (56, 60) sts.

Repeat *Rows 1 and 2* until 9 rows complete, ending on a repeat of *Row 1*. Continue to Back.

Back

Work in FLO for this section.

Row 1: Ch 2, dc in each st across second side, ch 36, dc in each st across first side of neck, turn—140 (148, 156) dc.

Row 2: Ch 1, sc in each st and ch across, turn.

Row 3: Ch 2, dc in each st across, turn.

Row 4: Ch 1, sc in each st across, turn.

Repeat *Rows 3 and 4* until 66 (68, 72) rows complete, ending on a repeat of *Row 4*.

Continue to Back Trim.

Back Trim

Ch 19.

Row 1: Sc in second ch from hook and in each ch across, sl st in next 2 sts of last row of Back, turn—18 sc, 2 sl sts.

Row 2: Skip 2 sl sts, BLO sc in each sc across, turn—18 sc.

Row 3: Ch 1, BLO sc in each sc across, sl st in next 2 sts of last row of back—18 sc, 2 sl sts.

Repeat *Rows 2 and 3* across the bottom back of Poncho, ending on a repeat of *Row 2*.

Continue to Side Trim.

Side Trim

Setup Row: Ch 1, sc evenly along the side of Poncho—224, (230, 242) sc.

Ch 7.

Row 1: Sc in second ch from hook and in each ch across, sl st in next 2 sts of Setup Row, turn—6 sc.

Row 2: Skip 2 sl sts, BLO sc in each sc across, turn—6 sc.

Row 3: Ch 1, BLO sc in each st across, sl st in next 2 sts of Poncho side—6 sc.

Repeat *Rows 2 and 3* along entire side of Poncho.

Fasten off. With RS facing, join yarn to bottom of second side. Repeat section for second Side Trim (both sides).

Neck Trim

Join yarn to any st of neck.

Setup Round: Ch 1, sc evenly around neck opening, sl st to first sc to join round—102 sc.

Ch 5.

Row 1: Sc in second ch from hook and in each ch across, sl st in next 2 sts of Setup Round, turn—4 sc.

Row 2: Skip 2 sl sts, BLO sc in each sc across, turn—4 sc.

Row 3: Ch 1, BLO sc in each st across, sl st in next 2 sts of Setup Round—4 sc.

Repeat *Rows 2 and 3* around neck opening; join last row to *Row 1* by slip stitching through both layers.

Fasten off.

Finishing

Block to measurements, weave in ends. If adding snaps, sew them on 13 (13.5, 14) in./33 (34, 35.5) cm from bottom of Front and 14 (14.5, 15) in./35.5 (37, 38) cm from bottom of Back. The Back should be 2 in./5 cm longer than the Front.

Stearns Poncho

Designed by Katy Petersen

Mandala yarn makes achieving the variety of colors in this poncho effortless, not to mention stunning. This oversize piece is very lightweight, seamless, and so much fun to wear!

SKILL LEVEL
Intermediate

SIZES/FINISHED MEASUREMENTS
Small/Medium (Large/1X, 2X/3X)
28 x 28 (30 x 29, 34 x 30) in./71 x 71 (76 x 73.5, 86.5 x 76) cm, laying flat
To fit shoulder width: 14–15 (16–17, 18–19) in./35.5–38 (40.5–43, 45.5–48) cm

YARN
Lion Brand Yarn Mandala, light weight #3 yarn (100% acrylic; 590 yd./540 m per 5.3 oz./150 g skein)
- 4 (4, 5) skeins Sphinx 216

HOOK AND OTHER MATERIALS
- US size G-6 (4.0 mm) crochet hook
- 2 size-4 snaps (optional)
- 1 stitch marker
- Yarn needle

GAUGE
18 exsc and 15 rows in pattern = 4 in./10 cm square (blocked)
Adjust hook size if necessary to obtain gauge.

SPECIAL STITCH
Exsc (extended single crochet). Insert hook into indicated stitch, yo and pull up a loop, yo and pull through 1 loop on hook, yo and pull through 2 remaining loops on hook.

NOTES
- Similar #3 weight yarns may be substituted; please check gauge.
- Poncho is worked in one piece. The Front is worked first, then the Split for the Neck, the Back, and finally the Trim.

INSTRUCTIONS

Front

Ch 109 (119, 137).

Row 1: Exsc in second ch from hook and in each ch across, turn—108 (118, 136) exsc.

Row 2: Ch 1, exsc in each st across, turn.

Repeat *Row 2* until 86 (90, 94) rows complete.

Split for Neck

First Side

Row 1: Ch 1, exsc in next 36 (41, 50), turn.

Repeat *Row 1* until 15 rows complete.

Fasten off.

Second Side

Skip 36 sts from First Side and join.

Repeat instructions from First Side.

Do not fasten off.

Back

Row 1: Ch 1, exsc in each st across, ch 36, exsc in each st of First Side of Split for Neck, turn.

Row 2: Ch 1, exsc in each st across, turn—108 (118, 136) exsc.

Repeat *Row 2* until 94 (98, 102) rows complete for Back.

Do not fasten off.

Body Trim

Round 1 (RS): Ch 1, rotate to work along Poncho side, exsc evenly across side (approx. 6 exsc for every 5 rows), 3 exsc in corner, rotate, exsc in each ch of beginning ch, 3 exsc in corner, rotate, exsc evenly across side of Poncho, 3 exsc in corner, rotate, exsc in each st of Back last row, 3 exsc in corner, place stitch marker to mark first st of round. Begin working in continuous rounds.

Rounds 2–9: Exsc in each st around working 3 exsc in each corner.

After Round 9: BLO sc in next st, sl st in next.

Fasten off.

Neck Trim

Round 1: With RS facing, join to any st of neck opening, ch 1, sc evenly around neck opening, place stitch marker to mark first st of round. Begin working in continuous rounds—108 sc.

Rounds 2–4: Ch 1, FLO sc in each st around.

Finishing

Fasten off and weave in ends. Block. To add optional snaps, sew on about halfway down side of Poncho, approximately 14 (14.5, 15) in./35.5 (37, 38) cm from bottom.

Light and Lacy Ruana

Designed by Cara Louise Reitbauer

This oversize design is a perfect layering piece without being too warm or heavy. The geometric, openwork pattern creates lace without being too frilly, and the softness of this yarn feels wonderful on bare skin.

SKILL LEVEL
Intermediate

SIZES/FINISHED MEASUREMENTS
One size; see notes for adjusting size.
Front section: 28 in./71 cm wide x 34 in./86.5 cm long from shoulder to bottom, excluding fringe

YARN
Lion Brand Yarn LB Collection Cotton Bamboo, light weight #3 yarn (52% cotton, 48% bamboo; 245 yd./224 m per 3.5 oz./100 g skein)
- 8 skeins Hyacinth 107

HOOK AND OTHER MATERIALS
- US size J-10 (6.0 mm) crochet hook
- Yarn needle

GAUGE
Gauge is not critical for this project.

SPECIAL STITCHES
Beginning LTR (beginning linked treble crochet). Insert hook in second ch from hook, yo and pull up loop, insert hook in third ch from hook, yo and pull up loop, skip 1 ch of foundation or first st at edge of row below, insert hook in next ch of foundation or next st of row below, yo and pull up loop (4 loops on hook), [yo and pull through 2 loops] 3 times.

LTR (linked treble crochet). Insert hook through top vertical bar of previous st, yo and pull up loop, insert hook through bottom vertical bar of same previous st, yo and pull up loop, insert hook in next unworked ch of foundation or next st of row below, yo and pull up loop (4 loops on hook), [yo and pull through 2 loops] 3 times.

Tr2tog (treble crochet 2 together). Yo twice, insert hook in first noted st or sp, yo and pull up loop, [yo and pull through 2 loops] twice (2 loops on hook), yo twice, insert hook in next noted st or sp, yo and pull up loop (5 loops on hook), [yo and pull through 2 loops] twice, yo and pull through last 3 loops on hook.

NOTES

- Similar #3 weight yarns may be substituted; please check gauge.
- The width of this design is suitable for an average Center Back Neck-to-Cuff length of about 30 in./76 cm. If a different finished width is desired, simply adjust the number of the starting chain. Each pattern repeat is approximately 2 in./5 cm wide and is worked over 8 sts. To adjust width, add or subtract 8 chs from beginning ch.
- The length of this design is designed to reach from the shoulders to above the knee, with the fringe then adding another 5.5 in./14 cm. To adjust for length, add or subtract rows as necessary, ending with a repeat of *Row 2*, before working *Last Row*.

INSTRUCTIONS

Front (make 2)

Ch 116.

Row 1 (RS): Beginning LTR, ch 3, skip 2 chs, sl st in next ch, ch 3, skip 2 chs, *tr in next 3 chs, ch 3, skip 2 chs, sl st in next ch, ch 3, skip 2 chs; repeat from * across to last 2 chs, tr in next ch, LTR in last ch, turn—13 groups of 3 tr; 2 LTR pairs; 52 ch-3 spaces.

Row 2 (WS): Ch 4 (counts as first tr), beginning LTR, ch 2, tr2tog over same st and next tr (skipping ch-spaces between), ch 2, *tr in same st and in next 2 tr, ch 2, tr2tog over same st and next tr, (skipping ch-spaces between), ch 2; repeat from * across row to last 2, tr in same st, LTR in top of turning ch, turn—13 groups of 3 tr, 2 LTR pairs, 52 ch-2 spaces.

Row 3 (RS): Ch 4, beginning LTR, ch 3, sc in space between 2 legs of tr2tog, ch 3, *tr in next 3 tr, ch 3, sc in space between 2 legs of tr2tog, ch 3; repeat from * across row to last 2, tr in same st, LTR in top of turning ch, turn—13 groups of 3 tr, 2 LTR pairs, 52 ch-3 spaces.

Repeat *Rows 2 and 3* ending with a repeat of *Row 2 (WS),* until 38 rows complete or until desired length from shoulder.

Last Row (RS): Ch 1, hdc in first 2 sts, 2 hdc in next space, hdc between 2 legs of tr2tog, 2 hdc in next space, *hdc in next 3 tr, 2 hdc in next space, hdc between 2 legs of tr2tog, 2 hdc in next space; repeat from * across row to last 2, hdc in last 2 sts—113 hdc. Fasten off.

Back

Hold first Front with starting chain at the top and the starting tail on the right side. Working in the remaining loop of beginning ch, join yarn to first st at edge, ch 4.

Row 1 (RS): Beginning LTR, ch 3, skip 2 chs, sc in next st of first Front, ch 3, skip 2 sts, *tr in next 3 chs, ch 3, skip 2 chs, sc in next st of first Front, ch 3, skip 2 chs; repeat from * across row of first Front, tr in next ch. Pick up second Front (with beginning foundation chain at the top and the starting tail on right side), LTR through last st of first Front and first st of second Front, LTR in next st of second Front, ch 3, skip 2 chs, sc in next st of second Front, ch 3, skip 2 chs, *tr in next 3 chs, ch 3, skip 2 chs, sc in next st of second Front, ch 3, skip 2 chs; repeat from * across row of second Front, tr in next ch, LTR in last ch, turn—26 groups of 3 tr, 1 group of 3 LTR in center, 2 LTR pairs at each end.

Row 2 (WS): Repeat *Row 2 of Front*—27 groups of 3 tr, 2 LTR pairs.

Row 3 (RS): Repeat *Row 3 of Front*—27 groups of 3 tr, 2 LTR pairs.

Repeat *Rows 2 and 3,* ending with a *Row 2 (WS),* until 38 rows complete or to match length of the 2 Front sections.

Last Row (RS): Repeat *Last Row of Front*—225 hdc.

Fringe

Cut 230 pieces of yarn 12 in./30.5 cm long. With RS of last row of first Front facing, insert hook through first st. Holding 2 strands together, fold in half, grab loop made at center of folded strands with hook, and pull loop through st; then use hook to pull all 4 tails of cut strands through loop, and tighten to secure. Skip 3 sts, attach fringe in similar fashion in next st. Continue across. Repeat on second Front and on Back.

Belt

Row 1: Ch 5, insert hook in second ch from hook, yo and pull up loop, insert hook in third ch from hook, yo and pull up loop, insert hook in fourth ch from hook, yo and pull up loop, insert hook in fifth ch from hook, yo and pull up loop (5 loops on hook), yo and pull through 1 loop (5 loops on hook), [yo and pull through 2 loops] 4 times.

Row 2: [Insert hook through vertical loop of next st, yo and pull up loop] 3 times, insert hook through 2 loops at edge of last ch, yo and pull up loop, yo and pull through 1 loop, (5 loops on hook), [yo and pull through 2 loops] 4 times.

Repeat *Row 2* until Belt is about 80 in./203 cm long, stretched (stretching amplifies the natural curl of this stitch pattern, which is perfect for a belt); fasten off.

Weave in all ends. Dampen all with warm water and lay flat on towels to dry, smoothing and opening up lace pattern.

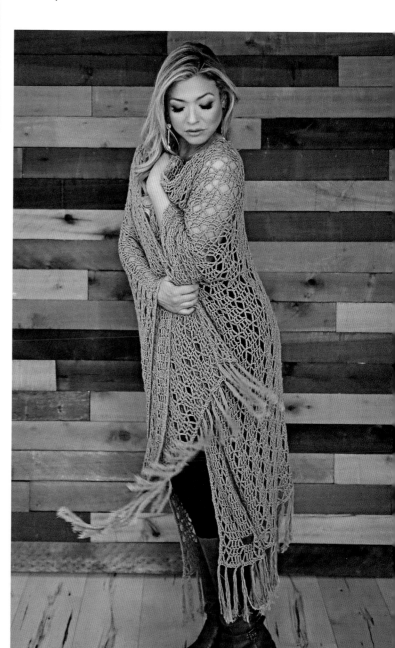

Mémé's Shawl

Designed by Cara Louise Reitbauer

This extravagantly long shawl is beautiful in its simplicity. The sparkle in this yarn is elegant, making a shawl that is perfect for a glamorous occasion, or even just a simple night out!

SKILL LEVEL
Intermediate

SIZES/FINISHED MEASUREMENTS
One size; see notes for adjusting size.
22 in./56 cm wide x 83 in./211 cm long

YARN
Lion Brand Yarn Vanna's Glamour fine weight #2 yarn (96% acrylic, 4% metallic polyester; 202 yd./185 m per 1.75 oz./50 g skein)
- 8 skeins Purple Topaz

HOOK AND OTHER MATERIALS
- US size G-6 (4.0 mm) crochet hook
- Yarn needle

GAUGE
Gauge is not critical for this project.

SPECIAL STITCH
Hdc2tog (half double crochet 2 stitches together) across same space and next space. Yo and insert hook in current space, yo and pull up loop (3 loops on hook), yo and insert hook in next space, yo and pull up loop (5 loops on hook), yo and pull through all loops on hook.

NOTES
- Similar #2 weight yarns may be substituted, but different yarn textures will result in different final results.
- Finished item is 6 pattern repeats wide. If a different finished width is desired, add or subtract 22 from the beginning chain to increase or decrease width by 1 repeat (about 4.5 in./11.5 cm).
- If a different finished length is desired, add or subtract repeats of *Rows 3–10*, to increase or decrease length by 2.75 in./7 cm.

▨ INSTRUCTIONS

Ch 112.

Row 1 (WS): Sc in second ch from hook and in each ch across, turn—111 sc.

Row 2 (RS): Ch 1, sc in first, [ch 5, skip 3 sts, sc in next] twice, *ch 3, skip 1 st, dc in next 3, ch 3, skip 1 st, sc in next, [ch 5, skip 3 sts, sc in next st] twice*, [ch 5, skip 3 sts, sc in next] twice; repeat from * across row, ending last repeat at *, turn—5 3-dc groups with 6 spaces between, 3 spaces at each end.

Row 3: Ch 5 (counts as dc, ch-2), *sc in next space, ch 5, sc in next space, ch 3, 2 dc in next space, dc in next 3 sts, 2 dc in next space, ch 3, sc in next space, ch 5, sc in next space*, ch 5; repeat from * across ending last repeat at *, ch 2, dc in last st, turn—5 7-dc groups with 5 spaces between, 3 spaces at each end.

Row 4: Ch 1, sc in first, skip 1 space, *ch 5, sc in next space, ch 3, 2 dc in next space, dc in next 3 sts, ch 3, skip 1 st, dc in next 3 sts, 2 dc in next space, ch 3, sc in next space, ch 5, sc in next space; repeat from * across, turn—5 pairs of 5-dc groups with 4 spaces between, 2 spaces at each end.

Row 5: Ch 5 (counts as dc, ch-2), *sc in next space, ch 3, 2 dc in next space, dc in next 3 sts, ch 3, sc in next space, ch 3, skip 2 sts, dc in next 3 sts, 2 dc in next space, ch 3, sc in next space*, ch 5; repeat from * across, ending last repeat at *, ch 2, dc in last st, turn—5 pairs of 5-dc groups with 3 spaces between, 2 spaces at each end.

Row 6: Ch 1, sc in first st, skip 1 space, *ch 3, 2 dc in next space, dc in next 3 sts, ch 5, skip 2 sts, sc in next st, ch 5, skip 2 sts, dc in next 3 sts, 2 dc in next space, ch 3, sc in next space; repeat from * across, turn—5 pairs of 5-dc groups with 2 spaces between, 1 space at each end.

Row 7: Ch 5 (counts as dc, ch-2), sc in next space, *ch 4, skip 2 sts, dc in next 3 sts, 2 dc in next space, ch 3, sc in next st, ch 3, 2 dc in next space, dc in next 3 sts, ch 4, sc in next space*, ch 5, sc in next space; repeat from * across ending last repeat at *, ch 2, dc in last st, turn—5 pairs of 5-dc groups with 3 spaces between, 2 spaces at each end.

Row 8: Ch 1, sc in first st, skip 1 space, *ch 5, sc in next space, ch 4, skip 2 sts, dc in next 3 sts, 2 dc in next space, ch 1, 2 dc in next space, dc in next 3 sts, ch 4, sc in next space, ch 5, sc in next space; repeat from * across row—5 pairs of 5-dc groups with 4 spaces between, 2 spaces at each end.

Row 9: Ch 5 (counts as dc ch-2), sc in next space, ch 5, sc in next space, *ch 4, skip 2 sts, dc in next 3 sts, dc in next space, dc in next 3 sts, ch 4, sc in next space, ch 5, sc in next space*, [ch 5, sc in next space] twice; repeat from * across ending last repeat at *, ch 2, dc in last st, turn—5 7-dc groups with 5 spaces between, 3 spaces at each end.

Row 10: Ch 1, sc in first st, skip 1 space, *[ch 5, sc in next space] twice, *ch 4, skip 2 sts, dc in next 3 sts, ch 4, sc in next space, [ch 5, sc in next space] twice; repeat from * across, turn—5 3-dc groups with 6 spaces between, 3 spaces at each end.

Repeat *Rows 3–10* another 29 times or until desired length is achieved.

Last Row: Ch 2, *[3 hdc in next space, hdc2tog across same space and next space] twice, hdc in same space, hdc in next 3 sts, hdc in next space, [hdc2tog across same space and next space, 3 hdc in same space] twice; repeat from * across to last, hdc in last st—111 hdc.

Fasten off.

Finishing

Weave in all ends. Dampen piece with warm water and lay flat on towels to dry, smoothing and opening up lace pattern.

Blue Boho Vest

Designed by Lee Sartori

This piece plays with color, stitch texture, and shape to create a chic look. Light, soft, and full of drape, this vest works on many levels and makes a fun statement piece!

SKILL LEVEL
Intermediate

SIZES/FINISHED MEASUREMENTS
Small (Medium, Large, 1X, 2X, 3X)
Width: 57 (58, 58.5, 59, 60, 61) in./145 (147, 149, 150, 152, 155) cm
Height: 26.5 in./67 cm (same for all sizes)

YARN
Lion Brand Yarn Jeans, medium weight #4 yarn (100% acrylic; 246 yd./225 m per 3.5 oz./100 g skein)
- 2 skeins Classic 110 (Color A)
- 2 skeins Stonewash 109 (Color B)
- 2 skeins Faded 105 (Color C)

HOOK AND OTHER MATERIALS
- US size I-9 (5.5 mm) crochet hook
- Yarn needle

GAUGE
14 dc and 8 rows = 4 in./10 cm
Adjust hook size if necessary to obtain gauge.

SPECIAL STITCH
Fdc (foundation double crochet). Ch 4 (beginning ch-3 counts as first dc), yo, insert hook in fourth ch from hook, yo and pull up loop (3 loops on hook), yo and pull through 1 loop (ch made), [yo and pull through 2 loops] twice (dc made), *yo, insert hook in ch of previous st, yo and pull up loop (3 loops on hook), yo and pull through 1 loop (ch made), [yo and pull through 2 loops] twice (dc made); repeat from * until required number of fdc have been made.

NOTES
- Similar #4 weight yarns may be substituted; please check gauge.
- Beginning ch counts as first st.
- Fasten off after every row, leaving 3 in./7.5 cm tails at each end.

INSTRUCTIONS

Row 1: With Color A, fdc 199 (202, 205, 208, 211, 214), turn.

Row 2: With Color B, ch 2 (counts as dc here and throughout), *skip 2 sts, 3 dc in next; repeat from * across row, dc into last st, turn—199 (202, 205, 208, 211, 214) sts.

Row 3: Ch 2, 2 dc in same st, *skip 2, 3 dc in space between next 2 dc; repeat from * across row, turn.

Row 4: Ch 2, skip 1, *3 dc in space between next 2 dc, skip 2; repeat from * across to last 3, skip 2, dc between last 2 dc, turn.

Rows 5–6: With Color C, repeat *Rows 3–4.*

Row 7: Repeat *Row 3.*

Row 8: With Color B, repeat *Row 4.*

Rows 9–10: Repeat *Rows 3–4.*

Row 11: With Color A, ch 2, dc in each st across, turn.

Row 12: Ch 3 (counts as dc, ch-1), skip 1, dc in next, *ch 1, skip 1, dc in next; repeat from * across, (omit last ch-1 for sizes Medium, 1X, 3X), turn—199 (201, 205, 207, 211, 213) dc.

Row 13: Ch 2, dc in each st across, turn.

Rows 14–15: With Color C, ch 4 (counts as tr, ch-1), skip 1, tr in next, *ch 1, skip 1, tr in next; repeat from * across, turn.

Row 16: With Color A, repeat *Row 13.*

Row 17: Ch 3 (counts as dc, ch-1), skip 1, dc in next, *ch 1, skip 1, dc in next; repeat from * across, turn.

Row 18: Ch 2, dc in each st across, (2 dc in last for sizes Medium, 1X, 3X), turn—199 (202, 205, 208, 211, 214) dc.

Row 19: With Color B, repeat *Row 4.*

Rows 20–21: Repeat *Rows 3–4.*

Rows 22–23: With Color C, repeat *Rows 3–4.*

Row 24: Repeat *Row 3.*

Row 25: With Color B, repeat *Row 4.*

Rows 26–27: Repeat *Rows 3–4.*

Rows 28–30: With Color A, repeat *Rows 11–13.*

Rows 31–32: With Color C, repeat *Rows 14–15.*

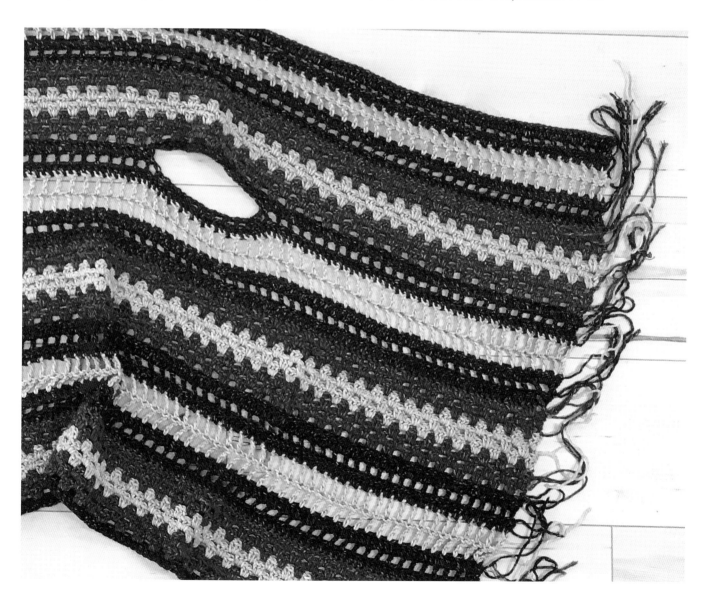

Rows 33–34: With Color A, repeat *Rows 11–12.*

Row 35: Ch 2, dc in next 58 (55, 49, 49, 49, 49), fdc 20 (20, 25, 25, 25, 25), dc in next 41 (50, 55, 58, 61, 64), fdc 20 (20, 25, 25, 25, 25), dc in next 59 (56, 50, 50, 50, 50), turn.

Rows 36–37: With Color B, repeat *Rows 3–4.*

Row 38: Repeat *Row 4.*

Row 39–40: With Color C, repeat *Rows 3–4.*

Row 41: Repeat *Row 3.*

Row 42: With Color B, repeat *Row 4.*

Rows 43–44: Repeat *Rows 3–4.*

Rows 45–47: With Color A, repeat *Rows 11–13.*

Rows 48–50: With Color C, repeat *Rows 14–15.*

Rows 51–53: With Color A, repeat *Rows 11–13.*

Fasten off and weave in ends (except fringe).

Goldenrod Cardigan

Designed by Lee Sartori

Everything about this cardigan is bold, from the color to the shape to the style and definitely the surprisingly simple construction! Once you put it on, you won't want to take it off.

SKILL LEVEL
Intermediate

SIZES/FINISHED MEASUREMENTS
Small (Medium, Large, 1X, 2X, 3X)
Width: 14 (21, 28, 35, 42, 49) in./35.5 (53, 71, 89, 106.5, 124.5) cm
Length: 38 (39, 40, 41, 42, 43) in./96.5 (99, 101.5, 104, 106.5, 109) cm

YARN
Lion Brand Yarn Jeans, medium weight #4 yarn (100% acrylic; 246 yd./225 m per 3.5 oz./100 g skein)
- 7 (7, 8, 8, 9, 10) skeins Top Stitch 121

HOOK AND OTHER MATERIALS
- US size H-8 (5.5 mm) crochet hook
- Yarn needle
- Stitch markers

GAUGE
14 BLO hdslst and 16 rows = 4 in./10 cm
Adjust hook size if necessary to obtain gauge.

SPECIAL STITCHES
Exsc (extended single crochet). Insert hook into indicated st, yo and pull up a loop, yo and pull through 1 loop on hook, yo and pull through 2 remaining loops on hook.

Fsc (foundation single crochet). Ch 2, insert hook in second ch from hook and pull up a loop, yo and pull through 1 loop on hook (ch made), yo and pull through 2 loops on hook (sc made), *insert hook in ch of previous st and pull up loop, yo and pull through 1 loop on hook (ch made), yo and pull through 2 loops on hook (sc made); repeat from * for required number of fsc.

Hdslst (half double slip stitch). Yo and insert hook in indicated st, yo, pull up loop and pull through 2 loops on hook.

NOTES

- Similar #4 weight yarns may be substituted; please check gauge.
- This piece is a long rectangle that, when sewed following Assembly directions, will become the final Cardigan. The sewing involves creating three seams.

INSTRUCTIONS

Body

Setup Row: Fsc 266 (273, 280, 287, 294, 301).

Row 1: Ch 2 (does not count as a st here and throughout), BLO hdslst in each st across, turn—266 (273, 280, 287, 294, 301) sts.

Rows 2–42 (63, 84, 105, 126, 147): Repeat *Row 1.*

Fasten off and weave in ends.

Assembly

Lay piece flat with long sides on top and bottom, short sides on the right and left. Fold left side across to right side (in half lengthwise). Starting from top right corners, sew piece one-third of the way shut across the top from edge toward fold. Place a stitch marker on each side of seam. This will form the seam going up and down the middle of the back. Find the center of the unsewn section and bring it down to meet the center back seam, forming a Y shape. Leaving 42 (44, 46, 48, 50, 52) sts unworked around top corners of the Y, sew horizontal seam across back. The remaining holes on each side become the Sleeves. Fasten off and weave in ends.

Sleeves

Join yarn in any st of armhole.

Round 1: Ch 1, exsc in each of the unworked 42 (44, 46, 48, 50, 53) sts of sleeve—42 (44, 46, 48, 50, 52) sts. Begin working in continuous rounds.

Rounds 2–52: Exsc in each st around.

Round 53: Sl st in next, ch 1, fpsc in each st around, sl st to first st to join.

Fasten off and weave in ends.

Collar

Join yarn in bottom left-hand corner of Body. Work in BLO.

Row 1: Ch 2 (does not count as a st here and throughout), hdslst in each across, turn—266 (273, 280, 287, 294, 301) sts.

Rows 2–12: Repeat *Row 1.*

Fasten off and weave in ends.

Sparkle Cocoon

Designed by Lee Sartori

The dazzling hint of sparkle in this yarn elevates a simple cocoon into a statement piece. Classic elegance like this can glam up an outfit year-round!

SKILL LEVEL
Intermediate

SIZES/FINISHED MEASUREMENTS
Small (Medium, Large, 1X, 2X, 3X)
Bust: Fits 28–32 (32–36, 36–40, 40–44, 44–48, 48–52)
   in./71–81 (81–91, 91–101.5, 101.5–112, 112–122,
   122–132) cm
Length: 30 (32, 34, 36, 38, 40) in./76 (81, 86.5, 91.5, 96.5,
   101.5) cm

YARN
Lion Brand Yarn Vanna's Glamour, fine weight #2 yarn
   (96% acrylic, 4% other; 202 yd./185 m per 1.75 oz./
   50 g skein)
   ▪ 7 (7, 8, 8, 9, 9) skeins Sapphire 109

HOOK AND OTHER MATERIALS
   ▪ US size G-6 (4.0 mm) crochet hook
   ▪ Yarn needle

GAUGE
8 rows of blocks = 4 in./10 cm
Adjust hook size if necessary to obtain gauge.

NOTE
   ▪ Similar #2 weight yarns may be substituted; please
     check gauge.

INSTRUCTIONS

Row 1: Ch 5, dc in third ch from hook (2 skipped chs count as ch-2 space), dc in next 2 chs, turn—1 block.

Increasing

Each row adds 1 block to stitch count.

Block Rows 2, 3, 4, 5: Ch 5, dc in third ch from hook (2 skipped chs count as ch-2 space here and through-out), dc in next 2 chs, *(sl st, ch 2, 3 dc) in next ch-2 space of previous row; repeat from * across, turn.

Eyelet Row 1: Ch 7, dc in seventh ch from hook, *sl st in next ch-2 space of previous row, ch 4, dc in next sl st; repeat from * across, work last dc in first ch of turning ch, turn.

Eyelet Rows 2, 3: Ch 7, dc in seventh ch from hook, *sl st in next ch-4 space of previous row, ch 4, dc in next sl st; repeat from * across to last space, (sl st, ch 4, dc) in last ch-7 space, turn.

Block Row 1 (first row after Eyelets): Ch 5, dc in third ch from hook, dc in next 2 chs, *(sl st, ch 2, 3 dc) in ch-4 space of previous row; repeat from * across to last ch-7 space, (sl st, ch 2, 3 dc) in last ch-7 space, turn.

Continue increasing in this manner, making 5 rows of Blocks followed by 3 rows of Eyelet blocks until there are 48 (53, 57, 62, 66, 70) blocks across.

Decreasing

Stitch count decreases by 1 block after each row.

49 Block #1 (54 Eyelet #1, 58 Block #2, 63 Eyelet #2, 67 Block #3, 71 Eyelet #2).

Block Rows 2, 3, 4, 5: Sl st across first 3 dc, *(sl st, ch 2, 3 dc) in next ch-2 space of previous row; repeat from * across to last ch-2 space, sl st in last space (do not make block in last space), turn.

Eyelet Row 1: Sl st across first 3 dc, *ch 4, dc in next sl st, *sl st in next ch-2 space, ch 4, dc in next sl st; repeat from * across to last ch-2 space, sl st in last space, turn.

Eyelet Rows 2, 3: Sl st across first 3 chs, *sl st in next ch-4 space of previous row, ch 4, dc in next sl st; repeat from * across to last space, sl st in last space (do not make block in last space), turn.

Block Row 1 (first row after Eyelets): Sl st across first 3 chs, *(sl st, ch 2, 3 dc) in ch-4 space of previous row; repeat from * across to last space, sl st in last space, turn.

Continue decreasing in this manner until 1 block remains. Fasten off and weave in ends.

Assembly

Fold piece in half. With yarn needle, sew together from top left corner, toward center approximately one-third of the way across. Join yarn at opposite corner, and sew together toward center approximately one-third of the way across. Fasten off and weave in ends.

Bottom Trim/Sleeve Cuffs

Row 1 (RS): Join yarn with sl st to bottom corner of Cardigan, ch 1 (not a st), hdc evenly across bottom of cardigan, turn.

Row 2: Ch 2 (counts as bphdc), bphdc in next, *fphdc in next 2, bphdc in next 2; repeat from *across, turn.

Rows 3–15: Repeat *Row 2.*

Fasten off and weave in ends.

Diamond Crop Top

Designed by Emily Truman

This summer top is designed for casual layering. Wear it over your suit at the beach, with a tank top in the summer, or paired with a taut spring dress!

SKILL LEVEL
Intermediate

SIZES/FINISHED MEASUREMENTS
Small (Medium, Large, 1X, 2X)
To fit bust measurement: 32 (36, 40, 44, 48) in./81 (91, 101.5, 112, 122) cm
Height: 17 (17, 18, 18, 19) in./43 (43, 45.5, 45.5, 48) cm after blocking
Panel: 21 (22, 23, 24, 25) in./53 (56, 58, 61, 63.5) cm

YARN
Lion Brand Yarn 24/7 Cotton, medium weight #4 yarn (100% cotton; 186 yd./170 m per 3.5 oz./100 g skein)
- 4 (4, 4, 5, 5) skeins Ecru 098

HOOK AND OTHER MATERIALS
- US size H-8 (5.0 mm) crochet hook
- Yarn needle

GAUGE
17 dc and 10 rows = 4 in./10 cm
Adjust hook size if necessary to obtain gauge.

SPECIAL STITCH
Shell. (2 dc, ch 1, 2 dc) in same st.

NOTES
- Similar #4 weight yarns may be substituted; please check gauge.
- Pattern is worked by making two panels and then sewing side seams and shoulder seams.

INSTRUCTIONS

Panel (make 2)

Ch 69 (73, 77, 81, 85).

Row 1: Dc in fourth ch from hook (skipped chs count as first dc), dc in next 6 (8, 10, 12, 14), ch 3, skip 1, sc in next, *ch 4, skip 3, sc in next; repeat from * across to last 7 (9, 11, 13, 15), ch 3, skip 1, dc in last 8 (10, 12, 14, 16) turn—16 (20, 24, 28, 32) dc, 12 ch-4 spaces, 2 ch-3 spaces.

Row 2: Ch 2 (counts as hdc here and throughout), hdc in next 7 (9, 11, 13, 15), sc in ch-3 space, *shell in next sc, sc in next ch-4 space, [ch 5, sc in next ch-4 space] 3 times; repeat from * twice more, shell in next sc, sc in ch-3 space, hdc in last 8 (10, 12, 14, 16), turn—16 (20, 24, 28, 32) hdc, 4 shells, 9 ch-5 spaces.

Row 3: Ch 2, hdc in next 7 (9, 11, 13, 15), 3 dc in next, *sc in ch-1 space of next shell, shell in next sc, sc in next ch-5 space, [ch 5, sc in next ch-5 space] twice, shell in next sc; repeat from * across, sc in ch-1 space of last shell, skip 2 dc, 3 dc in next, hdc in last 8 (10, 12, 14, 16), turn—16 (20, 24, 28, 32) hdc, 6 shells, 2 half shells, 6 ch-5 spaces.

Row 4: Ch 3 (counts as first dc here and throughout), dc in next 7 (9, 11, 13, 15), sc in next, shell in next sc*, sc in ch-1 space of next shell, [ch 5, sc in next ch-5 space] twice, ch 5, sc in ch-1 space of next shell; repeat from * across ending last repeat at **, skip 2 dc, sc in next, dc in last 8 (10, 12, 14, 16), turn—16 (20, 24, 28, 32) dc, 4 shells, 9 ch-5 spaces.

Row 5: Ch 2, hdc in next 7 (9, 11, 13, 15), ch 3, sc in ch-1 space of next shell, *[ch 5, sc in next ch-5 space] 3 times, ch 5, sc in ch-1 space of next shell; repeat from * across to last ch-1 space, ch 3, hdc in last 8 (10, 12, 14, 16), turn—16 (20, 24, 28, 32) hdc, 12 ch-5 spaces, 2 ch-3 spaces.

Row 6: Ch 2, hdc in next 7 (9, 11, 13, 15), sc in first ch-3 space, [ch 5, sc in next ch-5 space] 2 times, *shell in next sc, [sc in next ch-5 space, ch 5] 3 times, sc in next ch-5 space; repeat from * once more, shell in next sc, [sc in next ch-5 space, ch 5] 2 times, sc in next ch-5 space, hdc in last 8 (10, 12, 14, 16), turn—16 (20, 24, 28, 32) hdc, 3 shells, 10 ch-5 spaces.

Row 7: Ch 2, hdc in next 7 (9, 11, 13, 15), ch 3, sc in next ch-5 space, ch 5, sc in next ch-5 space, *shell in next sc, sc in ch-1 space of next shell, shell in next sc, sc in

next ch-5 space*, [ch 5, sc in next ch-5 space] twice; repeat from * across ending last repeat at *, ch 3, hdc in last 8 (10, 12, 14, 16), turn—16 (20, 24, 28, 32) dc, 6 shells, 6 ch-5 spaces, 2 ch-3 spaces.

Row 8: Ch 3, dc in next 7 (9, 11, 13, 15), sc in next ch-3 space, *ch 5, sc in next ch-5 space, ch 5, sc in ch-1 space of next shell, shell in next sc, sc in ch-1 space of next shell, ch 5, sc in next ch-5 space; repeat from * across, ch 5, sc in last ch-3 space, dc in last 8 (10, 12, 14, 16), turn—16 (20, 24, 28, 32) hdc, 3 shells, 10 ch-5 spaces.

Row 9: Ch 2, hdc in next 7 (9, 11, 13, 15), ch 3, sc in ch-5 space, ch 5, sc in next ch-5 space, *ch 5, sc in ch-1 space of next shell, [ch 5, sc in next ch-5 space] 3 times; repeat from * across once more, ch 5, sc in ch-1 space of next shell, [ch 5, sc in next ch-5 space] 2 times, ch 3, hdc in last 8 (10, 12, 14, 16), turn—16 (20, 24, 28, 32) hdc, 12 ch-5 spaces, 2 ch-3 spaces.

Row 10: Ch 2, hdc in next 7 (9, 11, 13, 15), sc in ch-3 space, *shell in next sc, sc in next ch-5 space, [ch 5, sc in next ch-5 space] 3 times; repeat from * twice more, shell in next sc, sc in next ch-3 space, hdc in last 8 (10, 12, 14, 16), turn—16 (20, 24, 28, 32) hdc, 4 shells, 9 ch-5 spaces.

Rows 11–36 (36, 40, 40, 44): Repeat *Rows 3–10*, ending on a repeat of *Row 4 (4, 8, 8, 4)*.

Small (Medium, 2X) only *Last Row (ending on a Row 4 repeat):* Ch 2, hdc in next 7 (9, 15), ch 2, sc in ch-1 space of next shell, *[ch 4, sc in next ch-5 space] 3 times, ch 4, sc in ch-1 space of next shell; repeat from * across to last ch-1 space, ch 2, hdc in last 8 (10, 16), turn—16 (20, 32) hdc, 12 ch-4 spaces, 2 ch-2 spaces.

Large (1X) only *Last Row (ending on a Row 8 repeat):* Ch 2, hdc in next 11 (13), ch 2, sc in ch-5 space, ch 5, sc in next ch-5 space, *ch 4, sc in ch-1 space of next shell, [ch 4, sc in next ch-5 space] 3 times; repeat from * across once more, ch 4, sc in ch-1 space of next shell, [ch 4, sc in next ch-5 space] 2 times, ch 2, hdc in last 12 (14), turn—24 (28) hdc, 12 ch-4 spaces, 2 ch-2 spaces.

Fasten off, leaving a long tail for sewing.

Shoulder Seam

With RS of both panels facing in, and with yarn needle and tail, sew both panels together from edge to second sc of openwork body section. Repeat for second shoulder. Fasten off.

Side Seam

Continue working on WS of garment. Join yarn with sc through both layers at side seam of waistline. Sc evenly through both layers to seam side for 10 (10, 10.5, 10.5, 11) in./25 (25, 27, 27, 28) cm. Fasten off and weave in all ends.

Olive Cardigan

Designed by Emily Truman

This cropped cardigan is anything but basic! The open stitchwork gives this piece a frilly design, but the olive color gives it a super-modern and elegant feel.

SKILL LEVEL
Intermediate

SIZES/FINISHED MEASUREMENTS
Small (Medium, Large, 1X, 2X)
Bust: 36 (40, 43, 46, 50) in./91 (101.5, 109, 117, 127) cm
Length: 19 (20, 20, 21, 21) in./48 (51, 51, 53, 53) cm

YARN
Lion Brand Yarn New Basic 175, medium weight #4
 yarn (75% acrylic, 25% wool; 175 yd./160 m per
 3.5 oz./100 g skein)
 - 4 (5, 5, 6, 6) skeins Olive 174

HOOK AND OTHER MATERIALS
 - US size I-9 (5.5 mm) crochet hook
 - Yarn needle
 - Stitch markers

GAUGE
Gauge swatch should measure 4 in./10 cm. Adjust hook
 size if necessary to obtain gauge. To make gauge
 swatch:
Ch 18.
Row 1 (RS): Sc in second ch from hook, [ch 2, skip 3, 4 tr
 in next, ch 2, skip 3, sc in next] twice, turn—2 groups
 of 4-tr.
Row 2 (WS): Ch 1, sc in same, [ch 3, sc in second tr of
 next 4-tr group, ch 3, sc in next sc] twice, turn—4
 ch-3 spaces.
Row 3: Ch 4 (counts as first tr), tr in same st, ch 2, sc in
 next sc, ch 2, 4 tr in next sc, ch 2, sc in next sc, ch 2, 3
 tr in last sc, turn—1 group of 4-tr, 2 half groups.
Row 4: Ch 1, sc in same, ch 3, sc in next sc, ch 3, sc in
 second tr of next 4-tr group, ch 3, sc in next sc, ch
 3, sc in fourth ch of beginning ch-4, turn—4 ch-3
 spaces.
Row 5: Ch 1, sc in same, [ch 2, 4 tr in next sc, ch 2, sc in
 next sc] twice, turn—2 groups of 4-tr.
Repeat *Rows 2–4.*

SPECIAL STITCH

3rd loop. Work sts into third loop of hdc behind front and back loops. When working in turned rows, the third loop is to the front of work.

NOTES

- Similar #4 weight yarns may be substituted; please check gauge.
- Pattern is worked in three rectangular panels. There are two smaller Front Panels and one larger Back Panel. The shoulders and sides are seamed and then the Border and Trim are added.

▌ INSTRUCTIONS

Front Panel (make 2)

Ch 34 (42, 42, 50, 50).

Row 1 (RS): Sc in second ch from hook, *ch 2, skip 3, 4 tr in next, ch 2, skip 3, sc in next; repeat from * across, turn—4 (5, 5, 6, 6) groups of 4-tr.

Row 2 (WS): Ch 1, sc in same, *ch 3, sc in second tr of next 4-tr group, ch 3, sc in next sc; repeat from * across, turn—8 (10, 10, 12, 12) ch-3 spaces.

Row 3: Ch 4 (counts as first tr), tr in same st, ch 2, *sc in next sc, ch 2, 4 tr in next sc, ch 2; repeat from * across to last 4-tr group, sc in next sc, ch 2, 3 tr in last sc, turn—3 (4, 4, 5, 5) groups of 4-tr, 2 half groups.

Row 4: Ch 1, sc in same, *ch 3, sc in next sc, ch 3, sc in second tr of next 4-tr group; repeat from * across, ch 3, sc in next sc, ch 3, sc in fourth ch of beginning ch-4, turn—8 (10, 10, 12, 12) ch-3 spaces.

Row 5: Ch 1, sc in same, *ch 2, 4 tr in next sc, ch 2, sc in next sc; repeat from * across, turn—4 (5, 5, 6, 6) groups of 4-tr.

Rows 6–38 (40, 40, 42, 42): Repeat *Rows 2–5* ending on a repeat of *Row 2 (4, 4, 2, 2).*

Back Panel

Ch 82 (82, 90, 98, 106).

Row 1 (RS): Sc in second ch from hook, *ch 2, skip 3, 4 tr in next, ch 2, skip 3, sc in next; repeat from * across, turn—10 (10, 11, 12, 13) groups of 4-tr.

Row 2 (WS): Ch 1, sc in same, *ch 3, sc in second tr of next 4-tr group, ch 3, sc in next sc; repeat from * across, turn—20 (20, 22, 24, 26) ch-3 spaces.

Row 3: Ch 4 (counts as first tr), tr in same st, ch 2, *sc in next sc, ch 2, 4 tr in next sc, ch 2; repeat from * across to last 4-tr group, sc in next sc, ch 2, 3 tr in last sc, turn—9 (9, 10, 11, 12) groups of 4-tr, 2 half groups.

Row 4: Ch 1, sc in same, *ch 3, sc in next sc, ch 3, sc in second tr of next 4-tr group; repeat from * across, ch 3, sc in next sc, ch 3, sc in fourth ch of beginning ch-4, turn—20 (20, 22, 24, 26) ch-3 spaces.

Row 5: Ch 1, sc in same, *ch 2, 4 tr in next sc, ch 2, sc in next sc; repeat from * across, turn—10 (10, 11, 12, 13) groups of 4-tr.

Rows 6–38 (40, 40, 42, 42): Repeat *Rows 2–5* ending on a repeat of *Row 2 (4, 4, 2, 2).*

Shoulder Seam

With RS facing in, lay Front Panels on top of Back Panel, so that side seams are aligned. Join yarn with a sc at corner, working through both layers, 3 sc through both ch-3 spaces across first Front Panel to make shoulder seam. Repeat for second Shoulder Seam and second Front Panel. Fasten off. Place stitch marker in top center stitch of Back Panel.

Side Seam

Count 5 (5, 5, 6, 6, 7) groups of 4-tr and mark stitch for armhole. Sc evenly up side seam working 4 sc in each tr row end and 1 sc in each sc row end. Fasten off, leaving a long tail. Repeat for second Side Seam.

Armhole

With RS facing, join yarn to bottom of Armhole. Working around Armhole, sc evenly around, working 4 sc for every 2 rows. Sl st to first sc to join. Fasten off. Repeat for second Armhole.

Border

Worked up and down front opening.

Row 1: With RS facing, join yarn to bottom right corner, ch 1, hdc evenly up right Front Panel, at stitch marker 2 hdc in next 2 sts, hdc evenly down left Front Panel, turn.

Row 2: Ch 1, 3rd loop hdc in each st across, working 2 hdc in 2 top sts, turn.

Row 3: Ch 1, BLO hdc in each st across, working 2 hdc in 2 top sts, turn.

Rows 4–9: Repeat *Rows 2–3.*

Ch 1, rotate to work along bottom and continue to Trim.

Bottom Trim

Worked in rows across bottom of piece.

Row 1 (RS): Join yarn to right side of piece at waistline, ch 1 (not a st), hdc evenly across working 4 hdc in each ch-space and 1 hdc in each st, turn.

Row 2: Ch 1, 3rd loop hdc in each st across, turn.

Row 3: Ch 1, BLO hdc in each st across.

Continue to Finishing.

Finishing

Rotate to work along neckline: 3rd loop sc across front panel neckline, ch 1 in corner, 3rd loop sc in each st across waistline, ch 1 at corner, sl st to first sc to join. Fasten off and weave in all ends.

Oversize Square Tee

Designed by Emily Truman

Comfy and oversize, this top is a casual addition to your wardrobe that complements so many body types. The sleeves are designed with a fitted cuff, making this top fit perfectly!

SKILL LEVEL
Intermediate

SIZES/FINISHED MEASUREMENTS
Small (Medium, Large, 1X, 2X)
Panel height: 21.5 (22.5, 23.5, 24.5, 25.5) in./54.5 (57, 59.5, 62, 64.5) cm
Panel width: 32.5 (34, 35.5, 37, 38.5) in./82.5 (86.5, 90, 94, 98) cm

YARN
Lion Brand Yarn LB Collection Superwash Merino, light weight #3 yarn (100% superwash merino; 306 yd./280 m per 3.5 oz./100 g skein)
- 6 (7, 8, 9, 10) skeins Mahogany 127

HOOK AND OTHER MATERIALS
- US size 7 (4.5 mm) crochet hook
- Yarn needle
- Sewing pins

GAUGE
16 hdc and 11 rows = 4 in./10 cm
Adjust hook size if necessary to obtain gauge.

SPECIAL STITCHES
Beginning star (beginning star stitch). Ch 3, pull up loop in second ch from hook, in third ch from hook, and in first 2 sts of row (5 loops on hook), yo and pull through all loops on hook.
Star st (star stitch). Ch 2, pull up loop in second ch from hook, in center of previous star, in last leg of previous star, and in next 2 sts (6 loops on hook), yo and pull through all loops on hook.

NOTES
- Similar #3 weight yarns may be substituted; please check gauge.
- Pattern is worked flat with two Panels and two rectangular Sleeves and then seamed.
- Pattern is an oversize, loose-fitting garment. For a custom fit, with arms outstretched, measure from elbow to elbow. Sleeves add approximately 3.5 in./9 cm for a three-quarter-length sleeve.

INSTRUCTIONS

Panel (make 2)

Ch 136 (142, 148, 154, 160).

Row 1 (RS): Hdc in second ch from hook and in each ch across, turn—135 (141, 147, 153, 159) hdc.

Row 2: Ch 2 (counts as bphdc), *fphdc around next, bphdc around next; repeat from * across to last 2, fphdc around next, hdc in last, turn—135 (141, 147, 153, 159) sts.

Rows 3–5: Ch 1, hdc in each st across, turn.

Row 6: Beginning star, star across to last st, ch 1, hdc in last st, turn—67 (70, 73, 76, 82) stars, 1 hdc.

Row 7: Ch 1, 2 hdc in each ch-1 space across, hdc in last st, turn—135 (141, 147, 153, 159) hdc.

Rows 8–11: Ch 1, hdc in each st across, turn.

Repeat *Rows 6–11* 10 (11, 11, 12, 12) more times—11 (12, 12, 13, 13) rows of star sts. Fasten off.

Shoulder Seam

Align last row of both Panels so RS is facing in. Join yarn to WS of both Panels along edge.

Ch 1, sc in next 50 (50, 54, 54, 58) sts through both Panels. Fasten off. Repeat for opposite Shoulder Seam.

Neckline

Join yarn at shoulder seam to RS of neckline. Working around remaining hole from Shoulder Seam, ch 1, *fphdc around next, bphdc around next; repeat from * around, sl st to first st to join. Fasten off.

Sleeve Panel (make 2)

Ch 55 (59, 63, 67, 71).

Row 1 (RS): Hdc in second ch from hook and in each ch across, turn—54 (58, 62, 66, 70) hdc.

Row 2: Ch 2 (counts as bphdc), *fphdc around next, bphdc around next; repeat from * across to last, fphdc around last, turn—54 (58, 62, 66, 70) sts.

Rows 3–14: Ch 1, hdc in each st across, turn—54 (58, 62, 66, 70) hdc.

Fasten off.

Finishing

Working on WS of pattern, use sewing pins to align star st rows to form side seam. Fold Sleeve in half lengthwise and pin in place. Leave Sleeve open for now. With yarn needle, sew Panels together, forming the side seam until armhole is reached. Sew Sleeve around armhole. Lastly, sew seam of Sleeve in place. Repeat for opposite side. Fasten off and weave in ends.

Tonal Pullover

Designed by Emily Truman

Pullovers are so easy to crochet, and they are even easier to wear. This style has a lot of texture to highlight the colors and tones in the yarn, creating a piece you'll love for many seasons!

SKILL LEVEL
Intermediate

SIZES/FINISHED MEASUREMENTS
Small (Medium, Large, 1X, 2X)
Front/Back Panel: 23 (24, 25.25, 26.5, 27.75) in./58 (61, 64, 67.5, 70.5) cm
Length: 17.5 (17.5, 18.5, 18.5, 19.5) in./44.5 (44.5, 47, 47, 49.5) cm

YARN
Lion Brand Yarn Wool-Ease Tonal, bulky weight #5 yarn (80% acrylic, 20% wool; 124 yd./113 m per 4 oz./ 113 g skein)
- 4 (5, 5, 6, 6) skeins Cabernet 189

HOOKS AND OTHER MATERIALS
- US size M-13 (9.0 mm) crochet hook
- US size L-11 (8.0 mm) crochet hook
- US size K-10½ (6.5 mm) crochet hook
- 2–4 buttons (1 in./2.5 cm)
- Yarn needle

GAUGE
With US M-13 (9.0 mm) hook, 10 sts and 7 pattern rows = 4 in./10 cm
Adjust hook size if necessary to obtain gauge.

NOTES
- Similar #5 weight yarns may be substituted; please check gauge.
- Pattern is worked with two rectangular Panels, seamed at the shoulders. Shaping is achieved while working the edging with a smaller hook size. Lastly, the Collar is worked with smaller hooks.

INSTRUCTIONS

Panel (make 2)

With US M-13 (9.0 mm) hook, ch 49 (53, 53, 53, 57).

Row 1: Dc in third ch from hook (skipped chs count as first st) and in each ch across, turn—48 (52, 52, 52, 56) dc.

Row 2: Ch 1 (not a st), BLO sl st in each st across, sl st in turning ch—48 (52, 52, 52, 56) sl sts.

Row 3: Ch 2 (counts as first dc here and throughout), BLO dc in each st across, turn.

Rows 4–35 (37, 39, 41, 43): Repeat *Rows 2–3*. Fasten off, leaving a long tail for seaming.

Shoulder Seam

Place RS of both Panels together with long tails at the top on opposite sides. With yarn needle and first tail, sew together both Panels for 8 (10, 10, 12, 12) rows (4 [5, 5, 6, 6] rows of dc) to seam shoulder. Fasten off. Repeat for opposite shoulder. Turn RS out.

Edging

Worked around entire piece.

With US L-11 (8.0 mm) hook, join yarn to RS of bottom corner of back Panel.

Round 1: Ch 1, *2 sc in each dc row end, 1 sc in each sl st row end*; repeat from * across bottom of back Panel, ch 1 at corner, sc in each st up back Panel and down

front Panel, ch 1 at corner, repeat from * to * across bottom front Panel, ch 1 at corner, sc in each st up front Panel and down back Panel, ch 1, sl st to first sc to join.

Round 2: Ch 1, BLO sc in each st around piece, (sc, ch 1, sc) in each corner ch-1 space, sl st to first sc to join.

Mark position for 2–4 buttonholes on front Panel as desired after Round 2 is complete. At each marker, ch 2, skip 2 sts, and continue pattern.

Round 3: Ch 1, BLO sc in each st and ch around piece, (sc, ch 1, sc) in each corner ch-1 space, sl st to first sc to join.

Change to US K-10½ (6.5 mm) hook.

Round 4: Ch 1, BLO sc in each st around piece, (sc, ch 1, sc) in each corner ch-1 space, sl st to first sc to join.

Fasten off.

Collar

With US L-11 (8.0 mm) hook, join yarn to inside Shoulder Seam.

Round 1: Ch 1, sc evenly around Collar, working 2 sc in each dc row end, and 1 sc in each sl st row end, sl st to first sc to join.

Rounds 2–4 (4, 4, 5, 5): Ch 1, BLO sc2tog, BLO sc in each st around to opposite Shoulder Seam, BLO sc2tog, BLO sc in each remaining st around, sl st to first sc to join.

Fasten off and weave in all ends.

Abbreviations

BLO	back loop only
bpdc	back post double crochet
bphdc	back post half double crochet
ch(s)	chain(s)
dc	double crochet
dc2tog	double crochet 2 stitches together
dc3tog	double crochet 3 stitches together
fdc	foundation double crochet
FLO	front loop only
fpdc	front post double crochet
hdc	half double crochet
hdc2tog	half double crochet 2 stitches together
RS	right side
sc	single crochet
sc2tog	single crochet 2 stitches together
sl st	slip stitch
st(s)	stitch(es)
tr	treble crochet
WS	wrong side
yo	yarn over
( )	work instructions within parentheses into stitch or space as directed
*	repeat instructions following or between asterisk(s) as directed
[]	work instructions within brackets as many times as directed

Designers

Create a free account to log on to Ravelry today; view all designs in this book, and meet the contributors!

Salena Baca | www.ravelry.com/people/SalenaBaca
Salena Baca has been hooked on crochet for more than twenty-five years and began designing in 2009. Salena is also the founder of several crochet organizations, including the American Crochet Association, where she works as the lead educator. She has filmed two classes with Craftsy and has published hundreds of patterns that you can find on Ravelry.

Ana Dyakova | www.ravelry.com/people/Accessorise
Raising her family and crocheting, Ana is loving life on the Danube River in Ruse, Bulgaria. She has a rich history in crafting, and her granny, mother, and aunt taught her to crochet, knit, sew, cross-stitch, and macrame. That history led her to open her first Etsy shop in 2011, and she has been writing and publishing her crochet patterns ever since. Crocheting is an inseparable part of her, and she loves combining this creativity with career goals in the business industry.

Julie King | www.ravelry.com/people/GleefulThings
Looking to fill the time that was once occupied by college work, Julie took an interest in crochet for the first time. With a little guidance from her mom and the internet, she was on her way. Julie started designing and selling her own crochet patterns in 2006, shortly after discovering Etsy. Having always been a craftsy person, designing came naturally to her. Even as a child, she enjoyed creating her own sewing patterns and craft projects. Originally specializing in amigurumi, Julie is now best known for her slouchy hats and "barefoot sandal" designs. Julie currently lives in Southern California, where she works as a crochet designer and blogger.

Toni Lipsey | www.ravelry.com/people/TLYarnCrafts
Toni is a crochet designer and instructor based in Columbus, Ohio, who's been creating since she was thirteen years old. An extrovert at heart, she loves planning knitting parties, teaching crochet lessons both in person and online, and attending local arts events. When she's not out and about, you can find her cuddling with her two kittens or designing new crochet patterns. Keep tabs on Toni via Instagram and visit TLYarnCrafts.com for her patterns and maker gifts.

Jess Mason | www.ravelry.com/people/ScreentoStitch
Jess Mason is the designer behind Screen to Stitch and the founder of the Yarnpreneur Society + Academy. She's been crocheting as a hobbyist for more than ten years, and she's been a yarnpreneur for five years. She loves designing, but more recently she's been spending more time helping yarnpreneurs build businesses they love. Her favorite things to do are crochet, read, and curl up with her kitty Cleo, who taunts her by sleeping all day!

Amber Millard | www.ravelry.com/people/divinedebris

Amber is a thirtysomething crochet fanatic. She enjoys yarn, coffee, and comic books, although not usually at the same time. Although she was taught to crochet at a young age, she didn't start crocheting until 2012, when she started creating her own jewelry. That hobby turned into blogging about her ideas and then full-time designing. She's been published in *Happily Hooked* magazine, in *Pattern Pack Pro*, and on Red Heart Yarns' website. She currently lives in North Carolina with her husband and their pet red-tailed boa.

Katy Petersen | www.ravelry.com/people/KTandtheSquid

Katy is the crochet and knitwear designer behind KT and the Squid. She taught herself to knit and crochet in high school and started designing in 2011. Her favorite things to make include garments and shawls for women. Her style is contemporary, lightweight, and simple. Katy is normally a quiet person, but if you get her talking about yarn, knit, or crochet, you'll never get her to stop. When she's not with her yarn, she enjoys laughing with her husband, three kids, and dog.

Cara Louise Reitbauer | www.ravelry.com/people/CaraLouise

Cara Louise has been crocheting since the age of eight, when her mother taught her with regular yarn and larger crochet hooks. A year or two later, she found a bag that had been her grandmother's, which contained some gorgeous doilies her grandmother had made, along with some skinny crochet thread and impossibly small steel crochet hooks. Cara fell in love at that first sight and created her very first doily that day by copying one of her grandmother's. When Cara crochets, she is honored and humbled to be able to follow in the crafting footsteps of both her mother and her grandmother.

Lee Sartori | www.ravelry.com/people/CoCoCrochetLee

Lee Sartori is the crochet designer behind CoCo Crochet Lee. She can be seen as a guest host on Season 9 of the popular PBS show *Knit and Crochet Now!*, as well as a cast member of *Annie's Creative Studio*, where she demonstrates fun crochet skills and patterns. Lee's passion is designing modern, wearable garments and adorable amigurumi. Lee lives in Ontario, Canada, with her two small children, her amazing husband, and her adorable bunny Neville. Her favorite social platform is Instagram, where she posts fun and whimsical takes on crochet.

Emily Truman | www.ravelry.com/people/Emilymtruman

Emily is the editor of *Happily Hooked* magazine and *Pattern Pack Pro* and the owner of Em's Corner. She spent her years before children as a middle school math teacher, but as a WAHM of four, she now enjoys crocheting at her kids' sporting events and spoiling her nieces and nephews. She loves teaching those nieces and nephews to crochet. When she's not crocheting, she's outside with her camera. She was raised in San Diego but now finds herself in the very hot Southern California desert.

Other Contributors

PATTERN TESTING

Melinda Edwards
Aleana Gallardo
Jenni Goodall
Vanessa Guida
Kelle Jones
Amanda Pippin
Jacqueline Powers
Sandy Powers
Jackie Ramsdell
Henrieke Ruane
Lindsey Strippelhoff
Hillary Thompson
Steff Walker
Susie Walker
Courtney Warriner
Michelle Wulf

TECHNICAL EDITOR

Emily Truman

SUPPORT

Lion Brand Yarn, LionBrand.com
Emily Gibbons Jewelry, EmilyGibbonsJewelry.com
Kaelin McDowell, KaelinMcDowellMakeup.com

PHOTOGRAPHY

Julie Lynn Photography, JulieLynnPhotos.com

MODELS

Emma Inwood
Marcella O'Campo
Amy Kaye

Acknowledgments

I always say that it takes a village to produce a book, and every single book I've made continues to bring in even more villagers! I owe so much thanks and gratitude to my ever-growing village!

My family has stood beside me at every step of my crochet career to cheer me on and encourage me. Without their love, I would not have the passion to do this work with a full heart.

Every one of the crochet pattern contributors in this collection is an individual I admire, respect, and value. Producing collections like this one is such a joy; working with the best and brightest continues to be a triumph that makes me so proud to serve the crochet community.

As an artist, you understand that even the best design can only truly be appreciated with vibrant models and a skilled photographer. I am extremely lucky to have both right here in my town. I thank them for always being kind, helpful, and supportive whenever I need them.

I am extremely grateful for Candi, and the entire Stackpole team, for trusting me to represent the needs of the crochet community. Their considerable support has been instrumental in ensuring that each collection we publish is something we're all proud of.

Peace + Love + Crochet
Salena

Visual Index

24/7 VEST   2

**COLD-SHOULDER
GRANNY SQUARE   6**

**FALLING LEAVES
SUPER SCARF   11**

**GRACEFUL GREEN
PONCHO   14**

**POUND OF LOVE
PONCHO   18**

BLANKET WRAP   21

**HEARTLAND
PONCHO   25**

FLOW PONCHO   29

**HEARTLAND
SHRUG 32**

**POINT THE WAY
PULLOVER 36**

XOXO KIMONO 40

ASTRID RUANA 44

**STONEWASHED
SHRUG 47**

**INVERTED TRIANGLES
SHRUG 51**

DIAMOND RUANA 56

PENNING PONCHO 62

STEARNS PONCHO 67

**LIGHT AND LACY
RUANA 71**

MÉMÉ'S SHAWL 76

BLUE BOHO VEST 81

**GOLDENROD
CARDIGAN 85**

SPARKLE COCOON 88

**DIAMOND
CROP TOP 92**

OLIVE CARDIGAN 96

**OVERSIZE
SQUARE TEE 100**

TONAL PULLOVER 104